CW00434313

The Top Air Fryer Cookbook UK 2023

The Quick & Easy and Yummy Air Fryer Meals for Beginners With Easy to Follow Instructions to Air Fry,Bake

Patsy M. Jasper

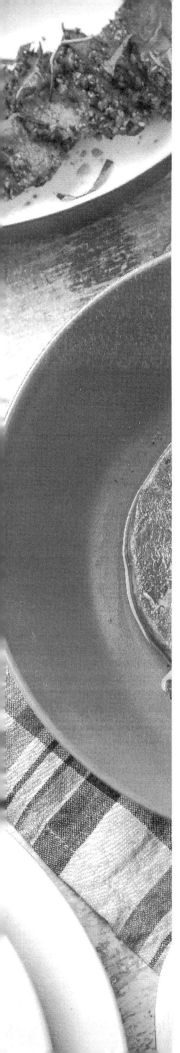

Contents

Introduction 1

Chapter 1

Breakfasts 10

Chapter 2

Fish and seafood 21

Chapter 3

Poultry 32

Chapter 4

Vegetables and Sides 41

Chapter 5

Beef, Pork, and Lamb 50

Chapter 6

Snacks and Appetisers 62

Chapter 7

Desserts 75

Air Fryer E-Book

Fish and chips, scotch eggs, fried chicken. For almost all of British history, the only way to have those foods would be if they were deep fried in oil (or lard in the past) bought from a takeaway shop.

Today, however, not only are people able to enjoy these, and many more, fantastic meals, we can do so for a fraction of the price and with a fraction of the saturated fat.

And that's possible because of the newest piece of kitchen tech- the air fryer! This book will look at what an air fryer is, why people love them so much, and what you can make with them.

Why I love my air fryer

Later in this book, I will go into far more detail about what I love so much about my air fryer, but in short, you can make delicious, quick, and healthy meals.

Restaurant quality food doesn't require much money on expensive cooking equipment or drowning your food in a deep fat fryer.

Even if you have a small kitchen, you can take your cooking to a new level with your air fryer.

As a professional chef, I work very hard in the kitchen all day, making some meals that took years of training. However, I don't want work to continue when I get home. I love throwing some fresh but simple ingredients into my air fryer and creating something magnificent.

What I hope this book will give you

Hopefully, by the end of this book, you will have the confidence to use your air fryer to make delicious and healthy meals. Be that healthy recreations of your favourite takeaways, traditional hearty meals, or new and adventurous dishes.

Yes, I am a professional chef with 20 years of experience, but you don't need to be. What I love about the air fryer is its simple and easy use!

After reading this book, I would encourage you to seek out new recipes or to try creating your own.

Getting to know the air fryer

The air fryer is an incredible piece of technology. Using just one spoonful of oil, you can create similar effects to a large tub of oil!

This chapter will examine how it works and why it's better than a deep fat fryer!

How does an air fryer work

An air fryer is essentially an enclosed convection oven.

Directly above your food is a heating element, which sends heat, via infrared radiation, downwards onto your food. But, what makes an air fryer different from a grill is the addition of the fan above the element.

The fan moves the hot air throughout the food- pushing hot air to the bottom, where it needs to pass through the food to rise to the top again.

An air guide (usually shaped like a starfish) at the

bottom of your air fryer distributes the hot air evenly. It ensures it reaches all parts of the food. The fact that your food is heated from all directions gives air-fried food a similar quality to fried foods. At the top, you'll find an exhaust, which releases a little air if the device gets too hot.

The (health) dangers of deep frying

Most people are aware that air frying uses significantly less fat than deep frying. But, have you ever wondered why fat is so bad for you?

Well, the truth is, not all fat is bad. But Trans Fats and saturated fats certainly are.

These fats increase your body's cholesterol- a thin layer of fat in our arteries. Cholesterol, in moderation, is essential for insulation. But, having too much of it can clog the arteries, stopping blood from travelling around your body.

Foods high in trans fats can't get broken down quickly, so they stick to your arteries and increase your cholesterol levels.

High cholesterol can lead to many medical issues, including heart disease, diabetes, and obesity.

As a mother, I want my kids to live long and happy lives. I certainly do not want them to live a life of clogged arteries.

Deep-fried foods are some of the worst for cholesterol. Foods are often fried in oils such as canola, soy, corn, sunflower, and sesame. Cheap oil is highly saturated and challenging for the body to break down.

Sure, you could fry in olive oil or similar oils, but could you imagine how much that would cost?

The (safety) dangers of deep frying

As well as health reasons, there are also safety reasons not to get a deep fat fryer.

Did you know deep fat fryers cause 1000 fires a year, with about 5 deaths... just on Thanksgiving! I couldn't even find the data for how much damage they cause in a year!

Here are some more reasons why you should opt for an air fryer over a deep fryer.

- It's more energy efficient. A deep fryer uses 1800 kWhs, but an air fryer only uses 1500.
- Your food cooks faster as you don't need to wait for lots of oil to heat up.

Food to cook and to avoid

Scotch Eggs

In many countries, most people aren't familiar with the "scotch egg", but when I visited the UK, I absolutely fell in love with them.

Essentially the scotch egg is an egg (as the name suggests) coated in sausage meat, covered in bread crumbs, and then deep fried (or air fried in my case).

It's a super simple yet delicious recipe that anyone can make. It uses everyday ingredients that most of us will have lying around.

And you can get creative with it too! For example, I once had a scotch egg that used panko bread crumbs and another that used black pudding instead of pork meat.

If you have an air fryer, you can have delicious, fresh, hot scotch eggs whenever you want.

Doughnuts

Doughnuts are a delicious sweet treat. Whether ringed or filled, a doughnut is a fantastic treat for anyone! Whether you're eating them on the go with a cup of coffee or sitting down to enjoy them.

The two main problems with doughnuts are how much they cost and how unhealthy they are. But, making your own in the air fryer eliminates both these problems.

Air fryer doughnuts are cheaper and healthier than you get in the doughnut shop.

Breaded fish

Fish is a delicious, high-protein food that goes well with many things. Breaded fish is best if you're cooking it in the air fryer.

Once you've cooked your breaded fish, you can serve it with fries, in a roll, or with vegetables. The choice is yours.

And don't think you have to use cod. There are many types of fish: halibut, salmon, mackerel, place, and huss. You could even cook whatever kind of fish is in your local area.

Chicken

We all love fried chicken. The juicy tender chicken is covered in a crispy breadcrumb. And now, you don't need to rely on greasy fast food joints or unhealthy frozen chicken to enjoy the delicious treat.

When you cook your "fried" chicken in the air fryer, it's healthier and often crispier than what you would get in fast food joints. Plus, you can use whatever herbs and spices you like.

Falafel

Falafel is a fantastic middle eastern food made from chickpeas. It's soft, flavoursome, and surprisingly healthy. Falafel has all the protein of a burger, with a tiny fraction of the saturated fat.

Whether you're vegetarian, trying to be healthy, or just want to explore new foods, falafel is a brilliant way to start!

Usually, it's served in balls, but you can also get falafel burgers.

Chips/Fries

Crispy on the outside, soft in the middle. Chips (or fries) are a favourite part of many people's diets. Nothing beats a nice hot bowl of chips with your favourite dipping sauce.

When you cook them in the air fryer, you get the chip's crispiness from the deep fryer, with just a tiny fraction of the fat.

Once they're cooked, you eat them just the same! Be that with a burger, fish, fried chicken, or coated in sauce.

Roast Potatoes

Staying with the theme of potatoes, you can also make excellent roast potatoes in your air fryer. Cover them in oil, rosemary, thyme, or whatever herbs you want, and throw them into your air fryer.

Cooking roast potatoes in the air fryer makes them crispier and cooks them quicker than they would in the oven. If you're only cooking for one, heating a whole oven to cook a portion of potatoes is a waste of time.

Calamari

Calamari is one of the best ways to enjoy squid! They're rings of squid meat coated in breadcrumbs, Squid, like most fish, is an excellent source of protein and very easy to cook with!

What not to cook in an air fryer

That was what you SHOULD cook. But here's a quick list of what you shouldn't cook and why.
Wet Batter- It doesn't set like it does in oil.

- Leafy Greens- They will burn and cook unevenly.
- Whole roast meats- Even if it fits, the bit by the heat sources will burn before the bottom is cooked.
- Cheese- Will burn and stick. It will be a nightmare to clean!
- Raw Grains- Air frying is dry cooking. If you cook dry grains, they will burn.
- Toast- The crumbs will blow everywhere, making the air fryer harder to clean.

Eight Benefits of an air fryer

If you don't yet have an air fryer and you're questioning if you should, this next chapter is for you! There are hundreds of reasons I love my air fryer, but in this chapter, I've picked the eight most important reasons to convince you to spend your money on an air fryer.

#1 It's much healthier.

We spoke in chapter one about why fat is bad for your arteries. But, when you air fry instead of deep fry, you use a tiny fraction of the oil you would use otherwise. Just one teaspoon is enough to cook your food to perfection.

In case you skipped chapter one, our body takes a long time to break down trans fats, which are commonly found in cooking oils. Since our body can't break it down, it stores the fat in the arteries, but too much, stopping the blood from flowing.

#2 Food becomes much Crispier.

We all love crispy food. Whether it's fries, chicken, scotch egg, or anything. It's always better when it has that lovely bit of bite. Cooking things in the oven is rarely the best way to make them crispy. It may get crispy on top, but the beautiful crispy coating is more difficult.

Have you tried making oven chips in the oven? They're never as crispy as you want them to be! Before the air fryer, deep frying was the only way to get crispy food.

Plus, the addition of the basket lets fat drip away, making your food even crispier.

#3 Air frying is quick.

When you're hungry, you want your food and you want it fast. The trouble with conventional cooking is that it often involves preheating.

Do you want to wait to heat up a whole oven? Or a tub of oil? I certainly don't.

Air frying is 30-50% quicker than cooking in an oven.

#4 There is less mess.

Many people (myself included) love cooking but hate washing up. Not even the air fryer can eliminate the need for washing up completely. However, it's much easier to clean than a traditional deep-fat fryer.

I have a friend who works in Mcdonald's, constantly complaining about how much work it is to clean a deep fryer.

A deep fat fryer needs to be cleaned regularly. The oil needs to get drained, and the trays must be scrubbed.

But, because the air fryer hardly uses any oil, cleaning is much simpler.

#5 It's much safer

Because the device is self-contained, there is no hot oil splashing. This means you won't need to worry about burning yourself or the oil splashing onto your kitchen.

Safety is super important. If you're deep frying and oil splashes onto your bare skin, you will be in great pain. In some cases, you may even require medical attention.

#6 It doesn't spread heat or odour

If you live in an apartment, the last thing you need is your whole house smelling like whatever you're frying. But, because the air fryer is enclosed, all the smells stay trapped.

#7 It's Smaller.

Most air fryers are about the size of a toaster. These can easily be set up on the kitchen counter.

No matter how small your kitchen is, you can use an air fryer. Its small size makes it great for all sorts of people- folk who travel a lot, folk in a caravan, folk in a small kitchen.

#8 It's easy to use.

All you need to do is set the time, set the temperature, and press "Start".

Then, just leave it alone. What you do whilst it's frying is up to you. Cook your sides, have a tea, write a poem. It's up to you.

There are, of course, plenty more benefits of an air fryer, but those are the eight I find most important.

Risks

As great as air fryers are, nothing in this world is perfect. So, even if you decide to buy one, there are some things you ought to be aware of.

Please be aware this chapter is not designed to discourage you from buying an air fryer; the pros far outweigh the cons. However, it's still important to be aware of the risks before making this kind of investment.

It could (still) create harmful compounds

When you cook certain foods at high temperatures, you create certain chemicals that can increase the risk of cancer and other health-related illnesses.

If you cook with cheaper, saturated fats, consuming lots of food from your air fryer can still damage your arteries. Because there is less oil than deep frying, the health risks are lessened, but they are not entirely eliminated.

Extra research is still needed into how healthy air-fried food is- although most will agree it's far healthier than deep frying.

It's not 100% guaranteed to be healthy

We discussed the "Tik Tok Air Fryer Chef" in the introduction. People throw processed junk into their air fryers, such as frozen meats, processed cheese, and high-sodium ingredients.

Cooking this kind of food in an air fryer is better than a deep fryer, but a nacho-coated ball of processed hamburger meat with American cheese inside is not healthy, even if it is cooked in an air fryer.

Burning food is easy

The air fryer cooks food at very high temperatures very quickly. The air fryer is your friend if you don't have much time.

However, because it gets so hot so quickly, burning food is too easy.

Unlike a traditional grill or frying pan, which allows you to see your food, the air fryer is enclosed and almost always opaque. By the time you notice the smell, it will be too late.

Air Fryers are Small

We said in the "benefits" chapter that an air fryer is small and compact. For some people, this will be beneficial, but it also makes the air fryer inappropriate for larger events (such as family gatherings) or for use in the hospitality industry (for example, if you own a cafe).

How to clean an air fryer

The old saying goes, "cleanliness is next to godliness" whether you believe that to be true or not, it's always important to keep your cooking equipment clean.

Not only does this look nicer, but it's also more hygienic and energy efficient, as the air fryer only needs to heat up your food, not the grime.

If you fail to clean your air fryer, it will leave a nasty smell whenever you cook, and in some cases, it could even start smoking.

Our advice would be to clean it after every use. If you leave it for too long, the dirt will become caked on and more difficult to clean.

How to clean an air fryer (Method #1)

1. Unplug your air fryer, leave it to cool, and start by wiping it down to remove the worst of the grime.

Please note when I say "leave it to cool", I mean cool enough to touch, not cool enough for the dirt to solidify.

2. Use warm soapy water and a soft cloth to take off the bits of food and grease. The best type of soap to use is probably dish soap as it's designed to be tough and take off lots of fat.

3. If stains on the basket are too stubborn, remove the basket, and leave it to soak in warm soapy water for an hour or two.

4. Use a wooden skewer to get into the nooks and crannies you cannot get into with the soft cloth. You could also use a thin cleaning brush, which you can buy from places such as Dollar Tree or Poundland.

5. Use a damp cloth to degunk the inside of your air fryer.

How to clean an air fryer (Method #2)

There is another method, although I'm not sure how well this method works. I've tried it myself and can't figure out why it went wrong. But, I've heard other people who use the same process, say it works a treat.

I'll leave you to decide whether this method is legit or just clickbait.

1. Add dish soap and water into your air fryer.
2. Allow it to cook for 5 minutes at a medium temperature.
3. Pour out the hot soapy mixture. As you pour it out, the bits of food will pour out with it.
4. Rinse out the air fryer with plain water.
5. Dry with a tea towel or kitchen towel.

By the way, my advice about cleaning after use, not just when you notice a smell, applies to almost everything in your kitchen, not just the air fryer.

If you don't clean your air fryer, expect your food to take longer, bacteria to fester, and your kitchen to begin smoking.

Tips and Tricks

To finish this e-book, I've compiled a list of some tips and tricks I've learnt from using my air fryer.

Make sure the basket is always clean.

We spoke about this in the previous chapter. When your air fryer is clean, it will be more hygienic and efficient.

Don't wait for the dirt to solidify, clean it as soon as it gets dirty.

If you use parchment paper, also use heat-safe magnets

Some recipes may require you to preheat your air fryer with a layer of parchment paper. The problem is that the parchment paper can get blown around because of the fan. The solution is simply to use 4 heat-safe magnets to keep the paper attached to the device.

Place foil at the bottom for easy cleaning.

If you're cooking with more oil than usual, add a sheet of aluminium foil below the basket. Fat will drop onto the basket instead of the air fryer. Once the fat has cooled, you can remove it easily.

Par Boil your vegetables.

If you put raw vegetables such as carrots, swede, or potatoes into your air fryer, they will burn on the outside before they have cooked inside.

Therefore, we recommend boiling them in water for 5 minutes.

Start using your air fryer asap.

Some people are worried they'll make awful meals or want to read some more recipe books before starting. Our advice is to use your air fryer on day one.

The only way to learn is from your mistakes, and you need to use your air fryer to make mistakes.

Don't start with expensive stuff.

If you're new to the air fryer, maybe don't use lots of expensive ingredients. Use cheap vegetables or french fries.

Once you're confident with what you're doing, you can start to use more expensive ingredients.

Don't take times and temperatures as gospel.

Whenever you read a time and temperature in a recipe, remember that the chef's fryer will likely be different from your own.

If you notice your food always burns, use less time than the recipe calls for. If it's never done, use more time.

You could also adjust the temperature. Trial and error is better than treating recipes like gospel.

Also, open and check on your food. Most air fryers are designed to automatically turn off when they're opened.

General Advice

- Use a wireless thermometer to make sure meat like chicken is safe to eat.
- Never put your air fryer on the stove.
- Buy a reusable spray bottle and fill it with your preferred oil.
- Use foil to lift soft foods.

Veggie Frittata

Prep time: 7 minutes
Cook time: 21 to 23 minutes
Serves 2

Ingredients:

- Avocado oil spray
- 30 g diced red bell pepper
- 4 large eggs
- ½ teaspoon dried thyme
- 30 g diced red onion
- 30 g finely chopped broccoli
- 85 g shredded sharp Cheddar cheese, divided
- Sea salt and freshly ground black pepper, to taste

Method:

1. Spray a pan well with oil. Put the onion, pepper, and broccoli in the pan, place the pan in the air fryer, and set to 176ºC. Bake for 5 minutes.
2. While the vegetables cook, beat the eggs in a medium bowl. Stir in half of the cheese, and season with the thyme, salt, and pepper.
3. Add the eggs to the pan and top with the remaining cheese. Set the air fryer to 176ºC. Bake for 16 to 18 minutes, until cooked through.

Mozzarella Bacon Calzones

Prep time: 15 minutes
Cook time: 12 minutes
Serves 4

Ingredients:

- 2 large eggs
- 250 g shredded Mozzarella cheese
- 4 slices cooked bacon, crumbled
- 125 g blanched finely ground almond flour
- 60 g cream cheese, softened and broken into small pieces

Method:

1. Beat eggs in a small bowl. Pour into a medium nonstick skillet over medium heat and scramble. Set aside.
2. In a large microwave-safe bowl, mix flour and MozzarellAdd cream cheese to the bowl.
3. Place bowl in microwave and cook 45 seconds on high to melt cheese, then stir with a fork until a soft dough ball forms.
4. Cut a piece of baking paper to fit air fryer basket. Separate dough into two sections and press each out into an 8-inch round.

5. On half of each dough round, place half of the scrambled eggs and crumbled bacon. Fold the other side of the dough over and press to seal the edges.

6. Place calzones on ungreased baking paper and into air fryer basket. Adjust the temperature to 176°C and set the timer for 12 minutes, turning calzones halfway through cooking. Crust will be golden and firm when done.

7. Let calzones cool on a cooking rack 5 minutes before serving.

Easy Cheesy Broccoli

Prep time: 6 minutes
Cooking time: 25 minutes
Serves 4

Ingredients:

- 42g grated yellow cheese
- and cut small florets
- 150g dried rosemary
- Salt and ground black pepper to taste
- 1 large-sized head of broccoli, stemmed
- 36ml canola oil
- 150g dried basil

Method:

1. Bring a medium pan filled with lightly salted water to a boil. Then, boil the broccoli florets for about 3 minutes.

2. Drain the broccoli florets well; toss them with the canola oil, rosemary, basil, salt, and black pepper.

3. Set your air fryer to 0 degrees F; arrange the seasoned broccoli in the cooking basket; set the timer for 17 minutes. Toss the broccoli halfway through the cooking process.

4. Serve warm, topped with grated cheese, and enjoy!

Cheesy Cauliflower "Hash Browns"

Prep time: 30 minutes
Cook time: 24 minutes
Makes 6 hash browns

Ingredients:

- 60 g 100% cheese crisps
- 1 (340 g) steam bag cauliflower, cooked according to package instructions
- 1 large egg   • 60 g shredded sharp Cheddar cheese   • ½ teaspoon salt

Method:

1. Let cooked cauliflower cool 10 minutes.

2. Place cheese crisps into food processor and pulse on low 30 seconds until crisps are finely ground.

3. Using a kitchen towel, wring out excess moisture from cauliflower and place into food

processor.

4. Add egg to food processor and sprinkle with Cheddar and salt. Pulse five times until mixture is mostly smooth.

5. Cut two pieces of baking paper to fit air fryer basket. Separate mixture into six even scoops and place three on each piece of ungreased baking paper, keeping at least 2 inch of space between each scoop. Press each into a hash brown shape, about ¼ inch thick.

6. Place one batch on baking paper into air fryer basket. Adjust the temperature to 192ºC and air fry for 12 minutes, turning hash browns halfway through cooking. Hash browns will be golden brown when done. Repeat with second batch.

7. Allow 5 minutes to cool. Serve warm.

Gold Avocado

Prep time: 5 minutes
Cook time: 6 minutes
Serves 4

Ingredients:

- 2 large avocados, sliced
- Salt and ground black pepper, to taste
- 2 eggs, beaten
- ¼ teaspoon paprika
- 60 g plain flour
- 125 g bread crumbs

Method:

1. Preheat the air fryer to 204ºC.
2. Sprinkle paprika, salt and pepper on the slices of avocado.
3. Lightly coat the avocados with flour. Dredge them in the eggs, before covering with bread crumbs.
4. Transfer to the air fryer and air fry for 6 minutes.
5. Serve warm.

Breakfast Meatballs

Prep time: 10 minutes
Cook time: 15 minutes
Makes 18 meatballs

Ingredients:

- 455 g ground herbed pork sausage meat
- ¼ teaspoon ground black pepper
- 30 g cream cheese, softened
- ½ teaspoon salt
- 60 g shredded sharp Cheddar cheese
- 1 large egg, whisked

Method:

1. Combine all ingredients in a large bowl. Form mixture into eighteen 1-inch meatballs.
2. Place meatballs into ungreased air fryer basket. Adjust the temperature to 204ºC and air fry

for 15 minutes, shaking basket three times during cooking. Meatballs will be browned on the outside and have an internal temperature of at least 64°C when completely cooked. Serve warm.

Baked Peach Oatmeal

Prep time: 5 minutes
Cook time: 30 minutes
Serves 6

Ingredients:

- Olive oil cooking spray
- 500 ml unsweetened almond milk
- 125 g nonfat plain Greek yogurt
- ½ teaspoon ground cinnamon
- 185 g diced peaches, divided, plus more for serving (optional)
- 250 g certified gluten-free rolled oats
- 60 g raw honey, plus more for drizzling (optional)
- 1 teaspoon vanilla extract
- ¼ teaspoon salt

Method:

1. Preheat the air fryer to 192°C. Lightly coat the inside of a 6-inch cake pan with olive oil cooking spray.
2. In a large bowl, mix together the oats, almond milk, honey, yogurt, vanilla, cinnamon, and salt until well combined.
3. Fold in 95 g peaches and then pour the mixture into the prepared cake pan.
4. Sprinkle the remaining peaches across the top of the oatmeal mixture. Bake in the air fryer for 30 minutes.
5. Allow to set and cool for 5 minutes before serving with additional fresh fruit and honey for drizzling, if desired.

Breakfast Pita

Prep time: 5 minutes
Cook time: 6 minutes
Serves 2

Ingredients:

- 1 whole wheat pita
- ½ shallot, diced
- 1 large egg
- ¼ teaspoon dried thyme
- 2 tablespoons shredded Parmesan cheese
- 2 teaspoons olive oil
- ¼ teaspoon garlic, minced
- ¼ teaspoon dried oregano
- ⅛ teaspoon salt

Method:

1. Preheat the air fryer to 192°C.
2. Brush the top of the pita with olive oil, then spread the diced shallot and minced garlic over

the pita.

3. Crack the egg into a small bowl or ramekin, and season it with oregano, thyme, and salt.
4. Place the pita into the air fryer basket, and gently pour the egg onto the top of the pita. Sprinkle with cheese over the top.
5. Bake for 6 minutes.
6. Allow to cool for 5 minutes before cutting into pieces for serving.

Breakfast Calzone

Prep time: 15 minutes
Cook time: 15 minutes
Serves 4

Ingredients:

- 185 g shredded Mozzarella cheese
- 30 g full-fat cream cheese
- 4 large eggs, scrambled
- 8 tablespoons shredded mild Cheddar cheese
- 60 g blanched finely ground almond flour
- 1 large whole egg
- 230 g cooked sausage meat, crumbled

Method:

1. In a large microwave-safe bowl, add Mozzarella, almond flour, and cream cheese. Microwave for 1 minute. Stir until the mixture is smooth and forms a ball. Add the egg and stir until dough forms.
2. Place dough between two sheets of baking paper and roll out to ¼-inch thickness. Cut the dough into four rectangles.
3. Mix scrambled eggs and cooked sausage together in a large bowl. Divide the mixture evenly among each piece of dough, placing it on the lower half of the rectangle. Sprinkle each with 2 tablespoons Cheddar.
4. Fold over the rectangle to cover the egg and meat mixture. Pinch, roll, or use a wet fork to close the edges completely.
5. Cut a piece of baking paper to fit your air fryer basket and place the calzones onto the baking paper. Place baking paper into the air fryer basket.
6. Adjust the temperature to 192ºC and air fry for 15 minutes.
7. Flip the calzones halfway through the cooking time. When done, calzones should be golden in color. Serve immediately.

Hole in One

Prep time: 5 minutes
Cook time: 6 to 7 minutes
Serves 1

Ingredients:

- 1 slice bread
- 1 egg
- 1 tablespoon shredded Cheddar cheese
- 1 teaspoon soft butter
- Salt and pepper, to taste
- 2 teaspoons diced ham

Method:

1. Place a baking dish inside air fryer basket and preheat the air fryer to 164ºC.
2. Using a 2½-inch-diameter biscuit cutter, cut a hole in center of bread slice.
3. Spread softened butter on both sides of bread.
4. Lay bread slice in baking dish and crack egg into the hole. Sprinkle egg with salt and pepper to taste.
5. Cook for 5 minutes.
6. Turn toast over and top it with shredded cheese and diced ham.
7. Cook for 1 to 2 more minutes or until yolk is done to your liking.

Banana-Nut Muffins

Prep time: 5 minutes
Cook time: 15 minutes
Makes 10 muffins

Ingredients:

- Oil, for spraying
- 60 g packed light brown sugar
- 1 large egg
- 95 g plain flour
- 1 teaspoon ground cinnamon
- 2 very ripe bananas
- 80 ml rapeseed oil or vegetable oil
- 1 teaspoon vanilla extract
- 1 teaspoon baking powder
- 60 g chopped walnuts

Method:

1. Preheat the air fryer to 160ºC. Spray 10 silicone muffin cups lightly with oil.
2. In a medium bowl, mash the bananas. Add the brown sugar, canola oil, egg, and vanilla and stir to combine.
3. Fold in the flour, baking powder, and cinnamon until just combined.
4. Add the walnuts and fold a few times to distribute throughout the batter.
5. Divide the batter equally among the prepared muffin cups and place them in the basket. You may need to work in batches, depending on the size of your air fryer.
6. Cook for 15 minutes, or until golden brown and a toothpick inserted into the center of a muffin comes out clean. The air fryer tends to brown muffins more than the oven, so don't be alarmed if they are darker than you're used to. They will still taste great.
7. Let cool on a wire rack before serving.

Bunless Breakfast Turkey Burgers

Prep time: 5 minutes
Cook time: 15 minutes
Serves 4

Ingredients:

- 455 g ground turkey sausage, skinned
- ¼ teaspoon ground black pepper
- 2 tablespoons mayonnaise
- ½ teaspoon salt
- 30 g seeded and chopped green bell pepper
- 1 medium avocado, peeled, pitted, and sliced

Method:

1. In a large bowl, mix sausage with salt, black pepper, bell pepper, and mayonnaise. Form meat into four patties.
2. Place patties into ungreased air fryer basket. Adjust the temperature to 188°C and air fry for 15 minutes, turning patties halfway through cooking. Burgers will be done when dark brown and they have an internal temperature of at least 76°C.
3. Serve burgers topped with avocado slices on four medium plates.

Broccoli-Mushroom Frittata

Prep time: 10 minutes
Cook time: 20 minutes
Serves 2

Ingredients:

- 1 tablespoon olive oil
- 60 g sliced brown mushrooms
- ½ teaspoon salt
- 6 eggs
- 185 g broccoli florets, finely chopped
- 30 g finely chopped onion
- ¼ teaspoon freshly ground black pepper
- 30 g Parmesan cheese

Method:

1. In a nonstick cake pan, combine the olive oil, broccoli, mushrooms, onion, salt, and pepper. Stir until the vegetables are thoroughly coated with oil. Place the cake pan in the air fryer basket and set the air fryer to 204°C. Air fry for 5 minutes until the vegetables soften.
2. Meanwhile, in a medium bowl, whisk the eggs and Parmesan until thoroughly combined. Pour the egg mixture into the pan and shake gently to distribute the vegetables. Air fry for another 15 minutes until the eggs are set.
3. Remove from the air fryer and let sit for 5 minutes to cool slightly. Use a silicone spatula to gently lift the frittata onto a plate before serving.

Bacon Muffin Sandwiches

Prep time: 5 minutes
Cook time: 8 minutes
Serves 4

Ingredients:

- 4 English muffins, split
- 4 slices cheese
- 8 bacon medallions
- Cooking spray

Method:

1. Preheat the air fryer to 188°C.
2. Make the sandwiches: Top each of 4 muffin halves with 2 slices of Canadian bacon, 1 slice of cheese, and finish with the remaining muffin half.
3. Put the sandwiches in the air fryer basket and spritz the tops with cooking spray.
4. Bake for 4 minutes. Flip the sandwiches and bake for another 4 minutes.
5. Divide the sandwiches among four plates and serve warm.

SPICY BEANS

Prep time : 5 mins   Cook time : 9 mins Serves 2

Ingredients:

- 1 tin Butter Beans
- ½ teaspoon Cayenne pepper
- 150g Cherry tomatoes, chopped
- 50 g Tomato Puree
- Salt and Pepper
- 1 teaspoon Cumin
- 1 teaspoon Paprika
- 1 small Red onion, finely chopped
- 1 teaspoon Olive Oil

Serve with:

- Piece of toast per person
- Sliced Avocado

Method:

1. Drain the beans in a sieve and rinse under a tap a few times until water runs clear.
2. Mix all ingredients together in a bowl. Ensure they are mixed well and everything is coated.
3. In an oven friendly bowl such as a 20cm cake tin add the bean mixture.
4. Place the oven friendly bowl in the air fryer basket and close and cook for 5 minutes at 190°c.
5. Open after 5 minutes and stir around with a spatula.
6. Close air fryer and cook further for 4 minutes.
7. Serve on a piece of toast with some sliced Avocado on top.

Sausage and Egg Breakfast Burrito

Prep time: 5 minutes
Cook time: 30 minutes
Serves 6

Ingredients:

- 6 eggs
- Cooking oil
- 60 g chopped green bell pepper
- 125 g salsa
- 60 g shredded Cheddar cheese
- Salt and pepper, to taste
- 60 g chopped red bell pepper
- 230 g ground chicken sausage
- 6 medium (8-inch) flour tortillas

Method:

1. In a medium bowl, whisk the eggs. Add salt and pepper to taste.
2. Place a skillet on medium-high heat. Spray with cooking oil. Add the eggs. Scramble for 2 to 3 minutes, until the eggs are fluffy. Remove the eggs from the skillet and set aside.
3. If needed, spray the skillet with more oil. Add the chopped red and green bell peppers. Cook for 2 to 3 minutes, until the peppers are soft.
4. Add the ground sausage to the skillet. Break the sausage into smaller pieces using a spatula or spoon. Cook for 3 to 4 minutes, until the sausage is brown.
5. Add the salsa and scrambled eggs. Stir to combine. Remove the skillet from heat.
6. Spoon the mixture evenly onto the tortillas.
7. To form the burritos, fold the sides of each tortilla in toward the middle and then roll up from the bottom. You can secure each burrito with a toothpick. Or you can moisten the outside edge of the tortilla with a small amount of water. I prefer to use a cooking brush, but you can also dab with your fingers.
8. Spray the burritos with cooking oil and place them in the air fryer. Do not stack. Cook the burritos in batches if they do not all fit in the basket. Air fry at 204ºC for 8 minutes.
9. Open the air fryer and flip the burritos. Cook for an additional 2 minutes or until crisp.
10. If necessary, repeat steps 8 and 9 for the remaining burritos.
11. Sprinkle the Cheddar cheese over the burritos. Cool before serving.

Creamy Cinnamon Rolls

Prep time: 10 minutes
Cook time: 9 minutes
Serves 8

Ingredients:

- 455 g frozen shortcrust pastry, thawed
- 95 g brown sugar
- 60 g butter, melted
- 1½ tablespoons ground cinnamon

Cream Cheese Glaze:
- 110 g cream cheese, softened
- 160 g powdered sugar
- 2 tablespoons butter, softened
- ½ teaspoon vanilla extract

Method:

1. Let the bread dough come to room temperature on the counter. On a lightly floured surface, roll the dough into a 13-inch by 11-inch rectangle. Position the rectangle so the 13-inch side is facing you. Brush the melted butter all over the dough, leaving a 1-inch border uncovered along the edge farthest away from you.
2. Combine the brown sugar and cinnamon in a small bowl. Sprinkle the mixture evenly over the buttered dough, keeping the 1-inch border uncovered. Roll the dough into a log, starting with the edge closest to you. Roll the dough tightly, rolling evenly, and push out any air pockets. When you get to the uncovered edge of the dough, press the dough onto the roll to seal it together.
3. Cut the log into 8 pieces, slicing slowly with a sawing motion so you don't flatten the dough. Turn the slices on their sides and cover with a clean kitchen towel. Let the rolls sit in the warmest part of the kitchen for 1½ to 2 hours to rise.
4. To make the glaze, place the cream cheese and butter in a microwave-safe bowl. Soften the mixture in the microwave for 30 seconds at a time until it is easy to stir. Gradually add the powdered sugar and stir to combine. Add the vanilla extract and whisk until smooth. Set aside.
5. When the rolls have risen, preheat the air fryer to 176ºC.
6. Transfer 4 of the rolls to the air fryer basket. Air fry for 5 minutes. Turn the rolls over and air fry for another 4 minutes. Repeat with the remaining 4 rolls.
7. Let the rolls cool for two minutes before glazing. Spread large dollops of cream cheese glaze on top of the warm cinnamon rolls, allowing some glaze to drip down the side of the rolls. Serve warm.

Herb-roasted Cauliflower

Prep time: 4 minutes
Cooking time: 20 minutes
Serves 4

Ingredients:

- 375g cauliflower florets
- 6g onion powder
- 6g thyme
- 6g rosemary
- 6g paprika
- 150g sesame oil
- 6g garlic powder
- 6g sage
- Sea salt and cracked black pepper to taste

Method:

1. Start by preheating your Air Fryer to 400 degrees F.
2. Toss the cauliflower with the remaining ingredients; toss to coat well.
3. Cook for 12 minutes, shaking the cooking basket halfway through the cooking time. They will crisp up as they cool. Bon appétit!

Air Fryer Pancakes With Blueberries

Prep time: 10 minutes

Cooking time: 14 minutes

Serves 4

Ingredients:

- 50g plain flour
- 2 eggs
- 1g salt
- 10g butter, melted and slightly cooled (melted)
- 75g milk, unsweetened vanilla or flavoured
- 100g blueberries

Method:

1. Preheat the air fryer to 270 degrees F. Pour the flour into a bowl and mix in the butter, eggs, milk, salt and vanilla or flavoured milk. Stir until it forms into a thin paste. Add more flour if the mixture is too runny.
2. Preheat pan on the stove and spray with oil. Lightly spoon mixture onto pan and cook until browned. Flip over and repeat with other side.
3. Add blueberries to the pancakes and enjoy.

Spinach Omelet

Prep time: 5 minutes

Cook time: 12 minutes

Serves 2

Ingredients:

- 4 large eggs
- 2 tablespoons peeled and chopped yellow onion
- 60 g shredded mild Cheddar cheese
- 30 g chopped fresh spinach leaves
- 2 tablespoons salted butter, melted
- ¼ teaspoon salt

Method:

1. In an ungreased round nonstick baking dish, whisk eggs. Stir in spinach, onion, butter, Cheddar, and salt.
2. Place dish into air fryer basket. Adjust the temperature to 160°C and bake for 12 minutes. Omelet will be done when browned on the top and firm in the middle.
3. Slice in half and serve warm on two medium plates.

Aged Macadamia Nut Salmon

Prep time: 6 minutes
Cooking time: 10 minutes
Serves 2

Ingredients:

- 227g salmon fillet, skin intact
- 75ml macadamia nuts
- 2.5ml honey

For Sauce

- 15ml butter
- 185ml soy sauce (kenji or shoyu)

- 5ml olive oil
- 15ml lemon juice

- 30ml honey
- 1 pinch freshly ground pepper

Method:

1. For sauce, add all the ingredients in a small bowl and mix until well combined.
2. Heat up the air fryer to 175 degrees Celsius (347 degrees Fahrenheit) and set the timer to 10 minutes.
3. Wash the salmon fillet and pat dry with a towel.
4. Coat the salmon fillet with olive oil, lemon juice and honey using your hands. Rub the mixture until completely absorbed. Sprinkle over some freshly ground pepper for seasoning.
5. Once the salmon has cooked; transfer to a plate and allow to rest for 10 minutes.
6. Add the sauce to the air fryer and mix well, cook until it thickens. Dish up and serve immediately.
7. Divide into two servings with some fresh vegetables of your choice.

Cheese Ravioli and Marinara Sauce

Prep time: 8 minutes
Cooking time: 25 minutes
Serves 4

Ingredients:

- 250g basil leaves, roughly chopped (or 1 tsp dried basil)
- 2.8g paprika but you can use
- 2g celery seeds
- 250ml tomato passata
- 1.3g pepper
- 6g garlic powder

- smoked paprika if desired
- 2g black pepper
- 4.5g salt
- 6g oregano, dried and finely chopped
- 375g cheese ravioli (or you can use your desired filling)

Method:

1. Combine salt, pepper and garlic powder in the air fryer-safe bowl then set aside. Place oregano and celery seeds in the air fryer-safe bowl and mix well until combined. Set aside.

2. Place paprika, black pepper and basil leaves in the air fryer-safe bowl and mix together. Set aside. In your air fryer, cook marinara sauce at 170C for 5 minutes or until reduced by half. Set aside.

3. Place ravioli in the air fryer-safe bowl, pour over some oil (if required) and cook at 170C for 10 minutes or until cooked through. After 10 minutes, add tomato passata to the bowl, drizzle over some oil (if required) and continue cooking until ravioli is cooked.

4. Place sauce in a serving bowl, add ravioli and serve with toasted brown rice or quinoa as a side dish.

Apple Cider Mussels

Prep time: 10 minutes
Cook time: 2 minutes
Serves 5

Ingredients:

- 910 g mussels, cleaned and debearded
- 1 teaspoon ground cumin
- 65 ml apple cider vinegar
- 1 teaspoon onion powder
- 1 tablespoon avocado oil

Method:

1. Mix mussels with onion powder, ground cumin, avocado oil, and apple cider vinegar.
2. Put the mussels in the air fryer and cook at 200ºC for 2 minutes.

Crab-Stuffed Avocado Boats

Prep time: 5 minutes
Cook time: 7 minutes
Serves 4

Ingredients:

- 2 medium avocados, halved and pitted
- ¼ teaspoon Old Bay seasoning
- 2 tablespoons mayonnaise
- 230 g cooked crab meat
- 2 tablespoons peeled and diced yellow onion

Method:

1. Scoop out avocado flesh in each avocado half, leaving ½ inch around edges to form a shell. Chop scooped-out avocado.

2. In a medium bowl, combine crab meat, Old Bay seasoning, onion, mayonnaise, and chopped avocado. Place ¼ mixture into each avocado shell.

3. Place avocado boats into ungreased air fryer basket. Adjust the temperature to 176ºC and air fry for 7 minutes. Avocado will be browned on the top and mixture will be bubbling when done. Serve warm.

Southern-Style Catfish

Prep time: 10 minutes
Cook time: 12 minutes
Serves 4

Ingredients:

- 4 (200 g) catfish fillets
- 1 tablespoon lemon juice
- 2 teaspoons Old Bay seasoning
- ¼ teaspoon ground black pepper
- 80 g heavy whipping cream
- 125 g blanched finely ground almond flour
- ½ teaspoon salt

Method:

1. Place catfish fillets into a large bowl with cream and pour in lemon juice. Stir to coat.
2. In a separate large bowl, mix flour and Old Bay seasoning.
3. Remove each fillet and gently shake off excess cream. Sprinkle with salt and pepper. Press each fillet gently into flour mixture on both sides to coat.
4. Place fillets into ungreased air fryer basket. Adjust the temperature to 204ºC and air fry for 12 minutes, turning fillets halfway through cooking. Catfish will be golden brown and have an internal temperature of at least 64ºC when done. Serve warm.

Smoky Prawn and Chorizo Tapas

Prep time: 15 minutes
Cook time: 10 minutes
Serves 2 to 4

Ingredients:

- 110 g Spanish (cured) chorizo, halved horizontally and sliced crosswise
- 230 g raw medium prawns, peeled and deveined
- 1 small shallot, halved and thinly sliced
- 1 tablespoon finely chopped fresh oregano
- ¼ teaspoon kosher or coarse sea salt
- 3 tablespoons fresh orange juice
- 1 tablespoon extra-virgin olive oil
- 1 garlic clove, minced
- ½ teaspoon smoked Spanish paprika
- ¼ teaspoon black pepper
- 1 tablespoon minced fresh parsley

Method:

1. Place the chorizo in a baking pan. Set the pan in the air fryer basket. Set the air fryer to 192ºC for 5 minutes, or until the chorizo has started to brown and render its fat.
2. Meanwhile, in a large bowl, combine the prawns, olive oil, shallot, garlic, oregano, paprika, salt, and pepper. Toss until the prawns are well coated.

3. Transfer the prawns to the pan with the chorizo. Stir to combine. Place the pan in the air fryer basket. Cook for 10 minutes, stirring halfway through the cooking time.
4. Transfer the prawns and chorizo to a serving dish. Drizzle with the orange juice and toss to combine. Sprinkle with the parsley.

Snapper Scampi

Prep time: 5 minutes
Cook time: 8 to 10 minutes
Serves 4

Ingredients:

- 4 (170 g) skinless snapper or arctic char fillets
- 3 tablespoons lemon juice, divided
- Pinch salt
- 2 tablespoons butter
- 1 tablespoon olive oil
- ½ teaspoon dried basil
- Freshly ground black pepper, to taste
- 2 cloves garlic, minced

Method:

1. Rub the fish fillets with olive oil and 1 tablespoon of the lemon juice. Sprinkle with the basil, salt, and pepper, and place in the air fryer basket.
2. Air fry the fish at 192°C for 7 to 8 minutes or until the fish just flakes when tested with a fork. Remove the fish from the basket and put on a serving plate. Cover to keep warm.
3. In a baking pan, combine the butter, remaining 2 tablespoons lemon juice, and garlic. Bake in the air fryer for 1 to 2 minutes or until the garlic is sizzling. Pour this mixture over the fish and serve

Chicken Casserole

Prep time: 30 minutes
Cook time: 30 minutes
Serves 4

Ingredients:

- 5 Boneless/Skinless chicken thighs
- 2 cloves of crushed garlic
- 2 tsp dehydrated mixed herbs
- 550g chopped carrots
- 175g frozen green beans
- 700ml chicken stock
- 45g chopped onion
- 1 tbsp flaxseed oil
- 2 Bay leaves
- 2 chopped celery stalks
- 175g broccoli
- 2 ¼ chicken gravy granules

Method:

1. Select the 'sear/sauté' function on the ninja foodi for 6 minutes
2. 0Pour in the flaxseed oil, followed by the onions
3. Once the onions have softened, toss in the chicken thighs

4. After the 6 minute cooking duration, turn the air fryer off and add the remainder of the ingredients, with the exception of the green veg
5. Change the ninja foodi applications for pressure set for 20 minutes
6. Revert back to the 'sear/sauté' function and toss in the green vegetables . All the ingredients to sear for 4 minutes
7. Add some gravy granules
8. Simmer the food content for another 3-4 minutes . Retrieve the casserole and serve

Prawns Scampi with Spicy Pepper Sauce

Prep time: 10 minutes
Cooking time: 15 minutes
Serves 4

Ingredients:

- 340g prawns, peeled, deveined and thawed
- 3g cloves garlic, minced fine
- 10g parsley leaves
- 10ml balsamic vinegar
- 15ml olive oil
- 20g red onion, diced small
- 10ml tomato paste

Method:

1. Combine the olive oil, garlic and onion in a medium size frying pan over medium heat. Cook until the onion shrinks and becomes translucent (approx 3-5 minutes).
2. Add the tomato paste and balsamic vinegar; combine until aromatic (approx 3 minutes).
3. Add the Prawns and cook for another minute.
4. Transfer to a large serving plate, sprinkle with parsley leaves, serve with lemon wedges on the side to squeeze over if desired.

Tilapia Sandwiches with Tartar Sauce

Prep time: 8 minutes
Cook time: 17 minutes
Serves 4

Ingredients:

- 185 g mayonnaise
- 1 dill pickle spear, finely chopped
- ¼ teaspoon salt
- 40 g plain flour
- 220 g panko bread crumbs
- 4 (170 g) tilapia fillets
- 4 soft subway rolls
- 2 tablespoons dried minced onion
- 2 teaspoons pickle juice
- ⅛ teaspoon freshly ground black pepper
- 1 egg, lightly beaten
- 2 teaspoons lemon pepper
- Olive oil spray
- 4 butter lettuce leaves

Method:

1. To make the tartar sauce, in a small bowl, whisk the mayonnaise, dried onion, pickle, pickle juice, salt, and pepper until blended. Refrigerate while you make the fish.
2. Scoop the flour onto a plate; set aside.
3. Put the beaten egg in a medium shallow bowl.
4. On another plate, stir together the panko and lemon pepper.
5. Insert the crisper plate into the basket and the basket into the unit. Preheat the unit by selecting AIR FRY, setting the temperature to 204°C, and setting the time to 3 minutes. Select START/STOP to begin.
6. Dredge the tilapia fillets in the flour, in the egg, and press into the panko mixture to coat.
7. Once the unit is preheated, spray the crisper plate with olive oil and place a baking paper liner into the basket. Place the prepared fillets on the liner in a single layer. Lightly spray the fillets with olive oil.
8. Select AIR FRY, set the temperature to 204°C, and set the time to 17 minutes. Select START/STOP to begin.
9. After 8 minutes, remove the basket, carefully flip the fillets, and spray them with more olive oil. Reinsert the basket to resume cooking.
10. When the cooking is complete, the fillets should be golden and crispy and a food thermometer should register 64°C. Place each cooked fillet in a subway roll, top with a little bit of tartar sauce and lettuce, and serve.

Air Fryer Tuna and Courgette Tortillas

Preparation time: 15 minutes
Cooking time: 30 minutes
Serves 4

Ingredients:

- 3.5g salt
- 1.3g sesame seeds, toasted and roughly chopped
- 1.3g paprika
- 50g green onions, chopped
- 2g soy sauce powder
- 1g cumin

- 2g black pepper
- 1.3g garlic, toasted and roughly minced
- 500g courgette, sliced into thin rounds
- 125ml tomato ketchup (or tomato puree)
- 2g paprika

Method:

1. Place salt, pepper and sesame seeds in the air fryer-safe bowl and mix well until combined. Set aside.
2. In your air fryer, add green onions with tomato ketchup to your air fryer-safe bowl and mix well. Add garlic, paprika and cumin to the bowl and stir until combined. Add courgette to the bowl and stir until well coated with tomato ketchup mixture. Set aside. Add tomatoes to a large bowl, add soy sauce and set aside.

3. In your air fryer, add tuna and courgette, pour over the tomato sauce mixture, drizzle over some water if required then cook at 170C for 12 minutes or until cooked through. Serve immediately with green salad and toasted brown rice or quinoa to serve as a side dish.

New Orleans-Style Crab Cakes

Prep time: 10 minutes
Cook time: 8 to 10 minutes
Serves 4

Ingredients:

- 160 g bread crumbs
- 1 teaspoon dry mustard
- 1 teaspoon freshly ground black pepper
- 2 large eggs, beaten
- 40 g minced onion
- Pecan Tartar Sauce, for serving
- 2 teaspoons Creole Seasoning
- 1 teaspoon salt
- 185 g crab meat
- 1 teaspoon butter, melted
- Cooking spray

Method:

1. Preheat the air fryer to 176°C. Line the air fryer basket with baking paper.
2. In a medium bowl, whisk the bread crumbs, Creole Seasoning, dry mustard, salt, and pepper until blended. Add the crab meat, eggs, butter, and onion. Stir until blended. Shape the crab mixture into 8 patties.
3. Place the crab cakes on the baking paper and spritz with oil.
4. Air fry for 4 minutes. Flip the cakes, spritz them with oil, and air fry for 4 to 6 minutes more until the outsides are firm and a fork inserted into the center comes out clean. Serve with the Pecan Tartar Sauce.

Crab Legs

Prep time: 5 minutes
Cook time: 15 minutes
Serves 4

Ingredients:

- 60 g salted butter, melted and divided
- ¼ teaspoon garlic powder
- 1.4 kg crab legs
- Juice of ½ medium lemon

Method:

1. In a large bowl, drizzle 2 tablespoons butter over crab legs. Place crab legs into the air fryer basket.
2. Adjust the temperature to 204°C and air fry for 15 minutes.
3. Shake the air fryer basket to toss the crab legs halfway through the cooking time.

4. In a small bowl, mix remaining butter, garlic powder, and lemon juice.

5. To serve, crack open crab legs and remove meat. Dip in lemon butter.

Tuna and Fruit Kebabs

Prep time: 15 minutes
Cook time: 8 to 12 minutes
Serves 4

Ingredients:

- 455 g tuna steaks, cut into 1-inch cubes
- 60 g large red grapes
- 2 teaspoons grated fresh ginger
- Pinch cayenne pepper
- 60 g canned pineapple chunks, drained, juice reserved
- 1 tablespoon honey
- 1 teaspoon olive oil

Method:

1. Thread the tuna, pineapple, and grapes on 8 bamboo or 4 metal skewers that fit in the air fryer.

2. In a small bowl, whisk the honey, 1 tablespoon of reserved pineapple juice, the ginger, olive oil, and cayenne. Brush this mixture over the kebabs. Let them stand for 10 minutes.

3. Air fry the kebabs at 188ºC for 8 to 12 minutes, or until the tuna reaches an internal temperature of at least 64ºC on a meat thermometer, and the fruit is tender and glazed, brushing once with the remaining sauce. Discard any remaining marinade.

4. Serve immediately.

Tuna with Roasted Garlic and Hazelnuts

Prep time: 10 minutes
Cooking time: 15minutes
Serves 4

Ingredients:

- 75ml of the stock from the hake
- 20g hazelnuts, chopped
- 200g tuna fillet, cut into 1 inch x 1/2 inch pieces
- 15g roasted and crushed garlic clove

Method:

1. Combine all of the stock ingredients in a bowl, making sure to whisk in the hake slice at the end. Set aside for 5 minutes to allow the flavours to amalgamate.

2. Preheat your air fryer to 370 degrees.

3. Skewer the fish and roast in the air fryer.

4. Remove the hake from the stock and reserve the stock to make a sauce or to drizzle over your food.

5. Mix the roasted garlic and hazelnuts in a small bowl until well incorporated and set aside (be

careful not to incorporate too much red pepper as this could alter the flavour).

6. Place the tuna on a plate and serve with brown rice, fresh salad, and roasted garlic hazelnuts.

Marinated Salmon Fillets

Prep time: 10 minutes
Cook time: 15 to 20 minutes
Serves 4

Ingredients:

- 60 g soy sauce
- 1 tablespoon brown sugar
- 1 teaspoon mustard powder
- ½ teaspoon freshly ground black pepper
- 4 (170 g) salmon fillets, skin-on

- 65 ml rice wine vinegar
- 1 tablespoon olive oil
- 1 teaspoon ground ginger
- ½ teaspoon minced garlic
- Cooking spray

Method:

1. In a small bowl, combine the soy sauce, rice wine vinegar, brown sugar, olive oil, mustard powder, ginger, black pepper, and garlic to make a marinade.
2. Place the fillets in a shallow baking dish and pour the marinade over them. Cover the baking dish and marinate for at least 1 hour in the refrigerator, turning the fillets occasionally to keep them coated in the marinade.
3. Preheat the air fryer to 188°C. Spray the air fryer basket lightly with cooking spray.
4. Shake off as much marinade as possible from the fillets and place them, skin-side down, in the air fryer basket in a single layer. You may need to cook the fillets in batches.
5. Air fry for 15 to 20 minutes for well done. The minimum internal temperature should be 64°C at the thickest part of the fillets.
6. Serve hot.

Sweet Tilapia Fillets

Prep time: 5 minutes
Cook time: 14 minutes
Serves 4

Ingredients:

- 2 tablespoons granulated sweetener
- 4 tilapia fillets, boneless

- 1 tablespoon apple cider vinegar
- 1 teaspoon olive oil

Method:

1. Mix apple cider vinegar with olive oil and sweetener.
2. Then rub the tilapia fillets with the sweet mixture and put in the air fryer basket in one layer. Cook the fish at 184°C for 7 minutes per side.

Air Fryer Cottage Pie

Prep time: 5 minutes Cooking time: 20 minutes
Serves 4

Ingredients:

- 2g salt
- 3g paprika
- 2.5g olive oil
- 1.5g white onion, finely chopped
- 2g pepper
- 1.5g nutmeg
- 2 (720g each) minced beef (or lamb)

Method:

1. Season mince with salt, pepper and paprika. Set aside.
2. Heat oil in a large frying pan over medium high heat.
3. Cook mince for 3 minutes until browned then set aside in a bowl.
4. Add white onion to the frying pan and cook until softened and lightly browned.
5. Return mince to the frying pan along with all other ingredients and stir well to combine.
6. Bring to the boil then reduce heat and simmer until thickened (approximately 10 minutes). Set aside.

Air Fryer Prawns Fajitas

Prep time: 10 minutes
Cooking time: 30 minutes
Serves 4

Ingredients:

- 450g chicken breast, thinly sliced into bite sized pieces
- 400g raw king prawns, peeled and deveined
- 1.7g black pepper
- 1.5g paprika (plus extra for sprinkling)
- 2.5g oregano, dried and finely chopped
- 1.7g cumin seed (plus extra for sprinkling)
- 2.7g chilli powder
- 2g salt
- 310ml tomato sauce or salsa
- 2.5g garlic powder

Method:

1. Preheat the air fryer to 180 degrees Celsius/350 degrees Fahrenheit. Once hot, place the chicken breast in a single layer on to a wire rack. Set aside for 5 minutes until white meat is no longer pink.
2. Add the tomato sauce and spices to a small bowl and mix to combine. Set aside for later.
3. Once the chicken is ready, add it and the prawns onto a large plate (or directly inside of the air fryer basket). Pour the tomato sauce and spices over the chicken and prawns and toss to combine.
4. Cook for 20 minutes. Serve with rice or quinoa, green vegetables and lemon wedges.

Oregano Tilapia Fingers

Prep time: 15 minutes
Cook time: 9 minutes
Serves 4

Ingredients:

- 455 g tilapia fillet
- 2 eggs, beaten
- 1 teaspoon dried oregano
- 60 g coconut flour
- ½ teaspoon ground paprika
- 1 teaspoon avocado oil

Method:

1. Cut the tilapia fillets into fingers and sprinkle with ground paprika and dried oregano.
2. Then dip the tilapia fingers in eggs and coat in the coconut flour.
3. Sprinkle fish fingers with avocado oil and cook in the air fryer at 188°C for 9 minutes.

Almond-Crusted Fish

Prep time: 15 minutes
Cook time: 10 minutes
Serves 4

Ingredients:

- 4 (110 g) fish fillets
- 30 g sliced almonds, crushed
- ⅛ teaspoon cayenne
- 95 g flour
- Oil for misting or cooking spray
- 95 g bread crumbs
- 2 tablespoons lemon juice
- Salt and pepper, to taste
- 1 egg, beaten with 1 tablespoon water

Method:

1. Split fish fillets lengthwise down the center to create 8 pieces.
2. Mix bread crumbs and almonds together and set aside.
3. Mix the lemon juice and cayenne together. Brush on all sides of fish.
4. Season fish to taste with salt and pepper.
5. Place the flour on a sheet of wax paper.
6. Roll fillets in flour, dip in egg wash, and roll in the crumb mixture.
7. Mist both sides of fish with oil or cooking spray.
8. Spray the air fryer basket and lay fillets inside.
9. Roast at 200°C for 5 minutes, turn fish over, and cook for an additional 5 minutes or until fish is done and flakes easily.

Honey Duck Breasts

Prep time: 10 minutes
Cooking time: 20 minutes
Serves 4

Ingredients:

- 1.5g salt
- 0.5g grated nutmeg
- 50ml honey
- scored to ensure a perfect shape
- 2g ground cinnamon
- 3g rosemary leaves
- 6 x 150g skin-on duck breasts,

Method:

1. Heat the air fryer to 190C. Combine honey, nutmeg, salt and cinnamon in an air fryer-safe bowl. Mix well to combine.
2. Add duck breast into the mixture and turn to coat evenly. Place duck breast in the air fryer basket in a single layer and cook at 170C for 15 minutes until cooked through.
3. Remove from the air fryer and allow to rest for 5 minutes.
4. Serve with potato mash and your favourite greens.

Bacon-Wrapped Stuffed Chicken Breasts

Prep time: 15 minutes
Cook time: 30 minutes
Serves 4

Ingredients:

- 10 g chopped frozen spinach, thawed and squeezed dry
- 30 g cream cheese, softened
- 30 g grated Parmesan cheese
- 1 jalapeño, seeded and chopped
- ½ teaspoon kosher or coarse sea salt
- 1 teaspoon black pepper
- 2 large boneless, skinless chicken breasts, butterflied and pounded to ½-inch thickness
- 4 teaspoons salt-free Cajun seasoning
- 6 slices bacon

Method:

1. In a small bowl, combine the spinach, cream cheese, Parmesan cheese, jalapeño, salt, and pepper. Stir until well combined.
2. Place the butterflied chicken breasts on a flat surface. Spread the cream cheese mixture

evenly across each piece of chicken. Starting with the narrow end, roll up each chicken breast, ensuring the filling stays inside. Season chicken with the Cajun seasoning, patting it in to ensure it sticks to the meat.

3. Wrap each breast in 3 slices of bacon. Place in the air fryer basket. Set the air fryer to 176°C for 30 minutes. Use a meat thermometer to ensure the chicken has reached an internal temperature of 76°C.

4. Let the chicken stand 5 minutes before slicing each rolled-up breast in half to serve.

Shaking Tarragon Chicken Tenders

Prep time: 10 minutes

Cooking time: 15 minutes

Serves 4

Ingredients:

- 125ml dried tarragon
- 450g chicken
- 75g butter
- Salt and pepper to taste

Method:

1. Preheat the air fryer to 390 F. Lay an X 12-inch cut of foil on a flat surface. Place the chicken on the foil, sprinkle the tarragon on both, and share the butter onto both breasts. Sprinkle with salt and pepper.

2 Loosely wrap the foil around the breasts to enable airflow. Place the wrapped chicken in the basket and cook for 1minutes. Remove the chicken and carefully unwrap the foil. Serve with the sauce extract and steamed veggies.

3.Serve and enjoy.

Chicken Breasts with Asparagus, Beans, and Rocket

Prep time: 20 minutes

Cook time: 25 minutes

Serves 2

Ingredients:

- 125 g canned cannellini beans, rinsed
- 1 garlic clove, minced
- Salt and ground black pepper, to taste
- 230 g asparagus, trimmed and cut into 1-inch lengths
- 2 (230 g) boneless, skinless chicken breasts, trimmed
- ¼ teaspoon paprika
- 60 g baby rocket, rinsed and drained
- 1½ tablespoons red wine vinegar
- 2 tablespoons extra-virgin olive oil, divided
- ½ red onion, sliced thinly
- ½ teaspoon ground coriander

Method:

1. Preheat the air fryer to 204°C.

2. Warm the beans in microwave for 1 minutes and combine with red wine vinegar, garlic, 1 tablespoon of olive oil, ¼ teaspoon of salt, and ¼ teaspoon of ground black pepper in a bowl. Stir to mix well.

3. Combine the onion with ⅛ teaspoon of salt, ⅛ teaspoon of ground black pepper, and 2 teaspoons of olive oil in a separate bowl. Toss to coat well.

4. Place the onion in the air fryer and air fry for 2 minutes, then add the asparagus and air fry for 8 more minutes or until the asparagus is tender. Shake the basket halfway through. Transfer the onion and asparagus to the bowl with beans. Set aside.

5. Toss the chicken breasts with remaining ingredients, except for the baby arugula, in a large bowl.

6. Put the chicken breasts in the air fryer and air fry for 14 minutes or until the internal temperature of the chicken reaches at least 76°C. Flip the breasts halfway through.

7. Remove the chicken from the air fryer and serve on an aluminum foil with asparagus, beans, onion, and rocket. Sprinkle with salt and ground black pepper. Toss to serve.

Crisp Paprika Chicken Drumsticks

Prep time: 5 minutes
Cook time: 22 minutes
Serves 2

Ingredients:

- 2 teaspoons paprika
- 1 teaspoon garlic powder
- ½ teaspoon salt
- 4 (140 g) chicken drumsticks, trimmed
- 1 spring onion, green part only, sliced thin on bias
- 1 teaspoon packed brown sugar
- ½ teaspoon dry mustard
- Pinch pepper
- 1 teaspoon vegetable oil

Method:

1. Preheat the air fryer to 204°C.

2. Combine paprika, sugar, garlic powder, mustard, salt, and pepper in a bowl. Pat drumsticks dry with paper towels. Using metal skewer, poke 10 to 15 holes in skin of each drumstick. Rub with oil and sprinkle evenly with spice mixture.

3. Arrange drumsticks in air fryer basket, spaced evenly apart, alternating ends. Air fry until chicken is crisp and registers 92°C, 22 to 25 minutes, flipping chicken halfway through cooking.

4. Transfer chicken to serving platter, tent loosely with aluminum foil, and let rest for 5 minutes. Sprinkle with spring onion and serve.

Thai-Style Cornish Game Hens

Prep time: 30 minutes
Cook time: 20 minutes
Serves 4

Ingredients:

- 20 g chopped fresh coriander leaves and stems
- 1 tablespoon soy sauce
- 8 garlic cloves, smashed
- 2 tablespoons lemongrass paste
- 2 teaspoons ground coriander
- 1 teaspoon ground turmeric
- 2 Cornish game hens, giblets removed, split in half lengthwise
- 60 g fish sauce
- 1 Serrano chilli, seeded and chopped
- 2 tablespoons sugar
- 2 teaspoons black pepper
- 1 teaspoon kosher or coarse sea salt

Method:

1. In a blender, combine the coriander, fish sauce, soy sauce, Serrano, garlic, sugar, lemongrass, black pepper, coriander, salt, and turmeric. Blend until smooth.
2. Place the game hen halves in a large bowl. Pour the cilantro mixture over the hen halves and toss to coat. Marinate at room temperature for 30 minutes, or cover and refrigerate for up to 24 hours.
3. Arrange the hen halves in a single layer in the air fryer basket. Set the air fryer to 204°C for 20 minutes. Use a meat thermometer to ensure the game hens have reached an internal temperature of 76°C.

Chicken Schnitzel Dogs

Prep time: 15 minutes
Cook time: 8 to 10 minutes
Serves 4

Ingredients:

- 60 g plain flour
- 1 teaspoon marjoram
- ½ teaspoon thyme
- 1 teaspoon lemon juice
- 125 g bread crumbs
- Oil for misting or cooking spray
- 4 slices Gouda cheese
- 60 g shredded Savoy cabbage
- ½ teaspoon salt
- 1 teaspoon dried parsley flakes
- 1 egg
- 1 teaspoon water
- 4 chicken breast fillets, pounded thin
- 4 whole grain hotdog buns
- 1 small Granny Smith apple, thinly sliced
- Coleslaw dressing

Method:

In a shallow dish, mix together the flour, salt, marjoram, parsley, and thyme.
2. In another shallow dish, beat together egg, lemon juice, and water.
3. Place bread crumbs in a third shallow dish.
4. Cut each of the flattened chicken fillets in half lengthwise.
5. Dip flattened chicken strips in flour mixture, then egg wash. Let excess egg drip off and roll in bread crumbs. Spray both sides with oil or cooking spray.
6. Air fry at 200°C for 5 minutes. Spray with oil, turn over, and spray other side.

7. Cook for 3 to 5 minutes more, until well done and crispy brown.
8. To serve, place 2 schnitzel strips on bottom of each hotdog bun. Top with cheese, sliced apple, and cabbage. Drizzle with coleslaw dressing and top with other half of bun.

Golden Chicken Cutlets

Prep time: 15 minutes
Cook time: 15 minutes
Serves 4

Ingredients:

- 2 tablespoons panko breadcrumbs
- ⅛ tablespoon paprika
- 2 large eggs
- 1 tablespoon parsley
- Cooking spray
- 30 g grated Parmesan cheese
- ½ tablespoon garlic powder
- 4 chicken cutlets
- Salt and ground black pepper, to taste

Method:

1. Preheat air fryer to 204°C. Spritz the air fryer basket with cooking spray.
2. Combine the breadcrumbs, Parmesan, paprika, garlic powder, salt, and ground black pepper in a large bowl. Stir to mix well. Beat the eggs in a separate bowl.
3. Dredge the chicken cutlets in the beaten eggs, then roll over the breadcrumbs mixture to coat well. Shake the excess off.
4. Transfer the chicken cutlets in the preheated air fryer and spritz with cooking spray.
5. Air fry for 15 minutes or until crispy and golden brown. Flip the cutlets halfway through.
6. Serve with parsley on top.

Pork Scratching Fried Chicken

Prep time: 30 minutes
Cook time: 20 minutes
Serves 4

Ingredients:

- 60 g buffalo sauce
- ½ teaspoon paprika
- ¼ teaspoon ground black pepper
- 4 (110 g) boneless, skinless chicken breasts
- ½ teaspoon garlic powder
- 60 g pork scratchings, finely crushed

Method:

1. Pour buffalo sauce into a large sealable bowl or bag. Add chicken and toss to coat. Place sealed bowl or bag into refrigerator and let marinate at least 30 minutes up to overnight.
2. Remove chicken from marinade but do not shake excess sauce off chicken. Sprinkle both sides of thighs with paprika, garlic powder, and pepper.
3. Place pork scratchings into a large bowl and press each chicken breast into scratchings to coat

evenly on both sides.

4. Place chicken into ungreased air fryer basket. Adjust the temperature to 204ºC and roast for 20 minutes, turning chicken halfway through cooking. Chicken will be golden and have an internal temperature of at least 76ºC when done. Serve warm.

Air Fryer Chicken Curry

Prep time: 10 minutes
Cooking time: 20 minutes
Serves 4

Ingredients:

- 4 x 115g skinless boneless chicken breasts
- 100ml Greek yogurt
- 50g spinach, roughly chopped
- 0.5g black pepper
- 300ml coconut milk
- 100ml tomato pure
- 1.5g salt
- 3g turmeric

Method:

1. Pour tomato puree, coconut milk and yogurts into an air fryer-safe bowl.
2. Season with salt, pepper and turmeric. Stir well to combine ingredients.
3. Place chicken breast into the air fryer basket in a single layer and cook at 170C for 10 minutes.
4. Remove from the air fryer and stir through chopped spinach and allow to stand for 30 seconds for the spinach to wilt slightly.
5. Serve chicken curry with rice or naan breads.

Smoky Chicken Leg Quarters

Prep time: 30 minutes
Cook time: 23 to 27 minutes
Serves 6

Ingredients:

- 125 ml avocado oil
- 1 teaspoon sea salt
- ½ teaspoon dried rosemary
- ½ teaspoon freshly ground black pepper
- 2 teaspoons smoked paprika
- 1 teaspoon garlic powder
- ½ teaspoon dried thyme
- 910 g bone-in, skin-on chicken leg quarters

Method:

1. In a blender or small bowl, combine the avocado oil, smoked paprika, salt, garlic powder, rosemary, thyme, and black pepper.
2. Place the chicken in a shallow dish or large sandwich bag. Pour the marinade over the chicken, making sure all the legs are coated. Cover and marinate for at least 2 hours or overnight.
3. Place the chicken in a single layer in the air fryer basket, working in batches if necessary. Set the air fryer to 204ºC and air fry for 15 minutes. Flip the chicken legs, then reduce the

temperature to 176°C. Cook for 8 to 12 minutes more, until an instant-read thermometer reads 72°C when inserted into the thickest piece of chicken.

4. Allow to rest for 5 to 10 minutes before serving.

Bacon Lovers' Stuffed Chicken

Prep time: 10 minutes
Cook time: 20 minutes
Serves 4

Ingredients:

- 4 (140 g) boneless, skinless chicken breasts, pounded to ¼ inch thick
- 2 (150 g) packages Boursin cheese (or Kite Hill brand chive cream cheese style spread, softened, for dairy-free)
- 8 slices thin-cut bacon
- Sprig of fresh coriander, for garnish (optional)

Method:

1. Spray the air fryer basket with avocado oil. Preheat the air fryer to 204°C.
2. Place one of the chicken breasts on a cutting board. With a sharp knife held parallel to the cutting board, make a 1-inch-wide incision at the top of the breast. Carefully cut into the breast to form a large pocket, leaving a ½-inch border along the sides and bottom. Repeat with the other 3 chicken breasts.
3. Snip the corner of a large sandwich bag to form a ¾-inch hole. Place the Boursin cheese in the bag and pipe the cheese into the pockets in the chicken breasts, dividing the cheese evenly among them.
4. Wrap 2 slices of bacon around each chicken breast and secure the ends with toothpicks. Place the bacon-wrapped chicken in the air fryer basket and air fry until the bacon is crisp and the chicken's internal temperature reaches 76°C, about 18 to 20 minutes, flipping after 10 minutes. Garnish with a sprig of coriander before serving, if desired.
5. Store leftovers in an airtight container in the refrigerator for up to 4 days. Reheat in a preheated 204°C air fryer for 5 minutes, or until warmed through.

Air Fryer Chicken Nuggets

Preptime: 5 minutes
Cooking time: 20 minutes
Serves 4

Ingredients:

- 4 (115g each) skinless boneless chicken breasts
- 2.2g parmesan cheese, grated
- (or other cut of chicken)
- 300ml coconut milk

- 1 egg white
- 1 lime, zest and juice
- 1.5g salt
- 2g sesame seeds, toasted and roughly chopped
- 2g garlic, toasted and roughly minced
- 100ml Greek yogurt
- 0.5g Sriracha sauce (optional)
- 1.3g pepper

Method:

1. Pour tomato puree, coconut milk and yogurts into an air fryer-safe bowl. Season with salt, pepper and turmeric. Stir well to combine ingredients.
2. Place chicken breast into the air fryer basket in a single layer and cook at 170C for 15 minutes or until cooked through.
3. Remove from the air fryer and set aside on a serving dish.
4. Whisk egg white in a large bowl until frothy. Pour over the chicken breasts and toss well to coat each chicken piece evenly.
5. In an air fryer-safe bowl, add chicken pieces with egg white and cook at 170C for 10 minutes or until lightly golden brown. Remove from the fryer and serve immediately.
6. To serve: divide chicken nuggets between four serving containers and store in the fridge for 4 hours to allow any excess moisture to be absorbed by the chicken.

Fried Chicken Breasts

Prep time: 30 minutes

Cook time: 12 to 14 minutes

Serves 4

Ingredients:

- 450 g boneless, skinless chicken breasts
- 95 g finely ground blanched almond flour
- ½ teaspoon sea salt
- 2 large eggs
- 190 ml dill pickle juice
- 95 g finely grated Parmesan cheese
- ½ teaspoon freshly ground black pepper
- Avocado oil spray

Method:

1. Place the chicken breasts in a sandwich bag or between two pieces of cling film. Using a meat mallet or heavy skillet, pound the chicken to a uniform ½-inch thickness.
2. Place the chicken in a large bowl with the pickle juice. Cover and allow to brine in the refrigerator for up to 2 hours.
3. In a shallow dish, combine the almond flour, Parmesan cheese, salt, and pepper. In a separate, shallow bowl, beat the eggs.
4. Drain the chicken and pat it dry with paper towels. Dip in the eggs and then in the flour mixture, making sure to press the coating into the chicken. Spray both sides of the coated breasts with oil.
5. Spray the air fryer basket with oil and put the chicken inside. Set the temperature to 204ºC and air fry for 6 to 7 minutes.

6. Carefully flip the breasts with a spatula. Spray the breasts again with oil and continue cooking for 6 to 7 minutes more, until golden and crispy.

Rosemary Honey Air-Fried Duck Breasts with Bacon

Prep time: 10 minutes
Cooking time: 15 minutes
Serves 4

Ingredients:

- 1.2g ground cinnamon
- 400g tin peach, drained and chopped
- ensure a perfect shape
- 3g black pepper
- 50g rindless smoked back bacon, cut into4 pieces each
- 0.5g Chinese five spice powder
- 4 x 150g duck breast, skin on, scored to
- 1.5g salt
- 2g ground nutmeg

Method:

1. Heat the air fryer to 190C.
2. Place duck breasts skin side down in the air fryer basket and cook at 170C for 15 minutes until cooked through. Remove from the air fryer and allow to rest for 5 minutes.
3. While duck breasts are cooking, make the sauce by placing peach, bacon and Chinese five spice powder into an air fryer-safe bowl and cook at 170C for 5 minutes.
4. Remove from the air fryer and combine with duck breasts.
5. Serve with rice or couscous.

Lemon Pepper Chicken Wings

Prep time: 8 minutes
Cooking time: 16 minutes
Serves 3

Ingredients:

- 454g chicken wings
- 75g olive oil
- 3g lemon pepper
- 3g salt , to taste

Method:

1. Add chicken wings to the large mixing bowl.
2. Add remaining ingredients over chicken and toss well to coat.
3. Place chicken wings in the air fryer basket.
4. Cook chicken wings for 8 minutes at 0 F.
5. Turn chicken wings to another side and cook for 8 minutes more.
6. Serve and enjoy.

Green Tomato Salad

Prep time: 10 minutes
Cook time: 8 to 10 minutes
Serves 4

Ingredients:

- 4 green tomatoes
- 1 large egg, lightly beaten
- 1 tablespoon Creole seasoning
- ½ teaspoon salt
- 60 g peanut flour
- 1 (140 g) bag rocket

Buttermilk Dressing:

- 250 g mayonnaise
- 2 teaspoons fresh lemon juice
- 1 teaspoon dried dill
- ½ teaspoon salt
- ½ teaspoon onion powder
- 125 g sour cream
- 2 tablespoons finely chopped fresh parsley
- 1 teaspoon dried chives
- ½ teaspoon garlic powder

Method:

1. Preheat the air fryer to 204ºC.
2. Slice the tomatoes into ½-inch slices and sprinkle with the salt. Let sit for 5 to 10 minutes.
3. Place the egg in a small shallow bowl. In another small shallow bowl, combine the peanut flour and Creole seasoning. Dip each tomato slice into the egg wash, then dip into the peanut flour mixture, turning to coat evenly.
4. Working in batches if necessary, arrange the tomato slices in a single layer in the air fryer basket and spray both sides lightly with olive oil. Air fry until browned and crisp, 8 to 10 minutes.
5. To make the buttermilk dressing: In a small bowl, whisk together the mayonnaise, sour cream, lemon juice, parsley, dill, chives, salt, garlic powder, and onion powder.
6. Serve the tomato slices on top of a bed of the arugula with the dressing on the side.

Air Fryer Kidney Beans

Prep time: 5 minutes
Cooking time: 15 minutes
Serves 4

Ingredients:

- 200g kidney beans (pintos)
- 20ml olive oil
- 1.5g salt
- 5g garlic
- 1 onion
- 75ml water

Method:

1. Wash and cover the kidney beans with boiling water to soften them.

2. Set aside for 10 minutes to cool. Drain thoroughly.
3. Cut the pinto beans into halves and toss with salt, pepper and oil before setting to Air Fry for 10 minutes at 250°F (121°C).
4. Add the onion and garlic. Stir until combined before serving.

Kohlrabi Fries

Prep time: 10 minutes
Cook time: 20 to 30 minutes
Serves 4

Ingredients:

- 910 g kohlrabi, peeled and cut into ¼ to ½-inch fries
- 2 tablespoons olive oil
- Salt and freshly ground black pepper, to taste

Method:

1. Preheat the air fryer to 204°C.
2. In a large bowl, combine the kohlrabi and olive oil. Season to taste with salt and black pepper. Toss gently until thoroughly coated.
3. Working in batches if necessary, spread the kohlrabi in a single layer in the air fryer basket. Pausing halfway through the cooking time to shake the basket, air fry for 20 to 30 minutes until the fries are lightly browned and crunchy.

Air Fryer Aubergine Parmesan

Prep time: 5 minutes
Cooking time: 10 minutes
Serves 4

Ingredients:

- 800g aubergine
- 10g garlic
- 3g salt
- 5g olive oil
- 60ml water
- 1 onion
- 6g parmesan cheese

Method:

1. Cut the aubergine lengthwise and skin them.
2. Slice the aubergine into halves and then into half inch thick slices.
3. Set the Air Fryer to 250°F (121°C) for 10 minutes.
4. Toss the slices with salt, pepper, oil and water if desired.
5. Toss them again before adding the remaining ingredients.
6. Place in a serving plate, if desired, and serve while hot.

Curried Fruit

Prep time: 10 minutes
Cook time: 20 minutes
Serves 6

Ingredients: to 8

- 125 g cubed fresh pineapple
- 230 g frozen peaches, thawed
- 2 tablespoons brown sugar
- 125 g cubed fresh pear (firm, not overly ripe)
- 1 (425 g) can dark, sweet, pitted cherries with juice
- 1 teaspoon curry powder

Method:

1. Combine all ingredients in large bowl. Stir gently to mix in the sugar and curry.
2. Pour into a baking pan and bake at 184°C for 10 minutes.
3. Stir fruit and cook 10 more minutes.
4. Serve hot.

Hasselback Potatoes with Chive Pesto

Prep time: 10 minutes
Cook time: 40 minutes
Serves 2

Ingredients:

- 2 medium russet potatoes
- 5 tablespoons olive oil
- Kosher or coarse sea salt and freshly ground black pepper, to taste
- 5 g roughly chopped fresh chives
- 2 tablespoons packed fresh flat-leaf parsley leaves
- 1 tablespoon chopped walnuts
- 1 tablespoon grated Parmesan cheese
- 1 teaspoon fresh lemon juice
- 1 small garlic clove, peeled
- 60 g sour cream

Method:

1. Place the potatoes on a cutting board and lay a chopstick or thin-handled wooden spoon to the side of each potato. Thinly slice the potatoes crosswise, letting the chopstick or spoon handle stop the blade of your knife, and stop ½ inch short of each end of the potato. Rub the potatoes with 1 tablespoon of the olive oil and season with salt and pepper.
2. Place the potatoes, cut-side up, in the air fryer and air fry at 192°C until golden brown and crisp on the outside and tender inside, about 40 minutes, drizzling the insides with 1 tablespoon more olive oil and seasoning with more salt and pepper halfway through.
3. Meanwhile, in a small blender or food processor, combine the remaining 3 tablespoons olive

oil, the chives, parsley, walnuts, Parmesan, lemon juice, and garlic and purée until smooth. Season the chive pesto with salt and pepper.

4. Remove the potatoes from the air fryer and transfer to plates. Drizzle the potatoes with the pesto, letting it drip down into the grooves, then dollop each with sour cream and serve hot.

Asparagus Fries

Prep time: 15 minutes
Cook time: 5 to 7 minutes per batch
Serves 4

Ingredients:

- 340 g fresh asparagus spears with tough ends trimmed off
- 2 egg whites
- 60 ml water
- 95 g Panko bread crumbs
- 60 g grated Parmesan cheese, plus 2 tablespoons
- ¼ teaspoon salt
- Oil for misting or cooking spray

Method:

1. Preheat the air fryer to 200ºC.
2. In a shallow dish, beat egg whites and water until slightly foamy.
3. In another shallow dish, combine panko, Parmesan, and salt.
4. Dip asparagus spears in egg, then roll in crumbs. Spray with oil or cooking spray.
5. Place a layer of asparagus in air fryer basket, leaving just a little space in between each spear. Stack another layer on top, crosswise. Air fry at 200ºC for 5 to 7 minutes, until crispy and golden brown.
6. Repeat to cook remaining asparagus.

Indian Aubergine Bharta

Prep time: 15 minutes
Cook time: 20 minutes
Serves 4

Ingredients:

- 1 medium aubergine
- 60 g finely minced onion
- 2 tablespoons fresh lemon juice
- ½ teaspoon kosher or coarse salt
- 2 tablespoons vegetable oil
- 60 g finely chopped fresh tomato
- 2 tablespoons chopped fresh coriander
- ⅛ teaspoon cayenne pepper

Method:

1. Rub the aubergine all over with the vegetable oil. Place the aubergine in the air fryer basket.

Set the air fryer to 204°C for 20 minutes, or until the aubergine skin is blistered and charred.

2. Transfer the aubergine to a large sandwich bag, seal, and set aside for 15 to 20 minutes (the aubergine will finish cooking in the residual heat trapped in the bag).

3. Transfer the aubergine to a large bowl. Peel off and discard the charred skin. Roughly mash the aubergine flesh. Add the onion, tomato, lemon juice, coriander, salt, and cayenne. Stir to combine.

Spiced Butternut Squash

Prep time: 10 minutes
Cook time: 15 minutes
Serves 4

Ingredients:

- 500 g 1-inch-cubed butternut squash
- 1 to 2 tablespoons brown sugar
- 2 tablespoons vegetable oil
- 1 teaspoon Chinese five-spice powder

Method:

1. In a medium bowl, combine the squash, oil, sugar, and five-spice powder. Toss to coat.
2. Place the squash in the air fryer basket. Set the air fryer to 204°C for 15 minutes or until tender.

Roasted Brussels Sprouts with Bacon

Prep time: 10 minutes
Cook time: 20 minutes
Serves 4

Ingredients:

- 4 slices thick-cut bacon, chopped (about 115 g)
- 450 g Brussels sprouts, halved (or quartered if large)
- Freshly ground black pepper, to taste

Method:

1. Preheat the air fryer to 192°C.
2. Air fry the bacon for 5 minutes, shaking the basket once or twice during the cooking time.
3. Add the Brussels sprouts to the basket and drizzle a little bacon fat from the bottom of the air fryer drawer into the basket. Toss the sprouts to coat with the bacon fat. Air fry for an additional 15 minutes, or until the Brussels sprouts are tender to a knifepoint.
4. Season with freshly ground black pepper.

Roasted Sweet Potatoes

Prep time: 10 minutes

Cook time: 25 minutes
Serves 4

Ingredients:

- Cooking oil spray
- 1 tablespoon extra-virgin olive oil
- Freshly ground black pepper, to taste
- ½ teaspoon dried marjoram
- 2 sweet potatoes, peeled and cut into 1-inch cubes
- Pinch salt
- ½ teaspoon dried thyme
- 30 g grated Parmesan cheese

Method:

1. Insert the crisper plate into the basket and the basket into the unit. Preheat the unit by selecting AIR ROAST, setting the temperature to 164ºC, and setting the time to 3 minutes. Select START/STOP to begin.
2. Once the unit is preheated, spray the crisper plate with cooking oil. Put the sweet potato cubes into the basket and drizzle with olive oil. Toss gently to coat. Sprinkle with the salt, pepper, thyme, and marjoram and toss again.
3. Select AIR ROAST, set the temperature to 164ºC, and set the time to 25 minutes. Select START/STOP to begin.
4. After 10 minutes, remove the basket and shake the potatoes. Reinsert the basket to resume cooking. After another 10 minutes, remove the basket and shake the potatoes one more time. Sprinkle evenly with the Parmesan cheese. Reinsert the basket to resume cooking.
5. When the cooking is complete, the potatoes should be tender. Serve immediately.

Radish Chips

Prep time: 10 minutes
Cook time: 5 minutes
Serves 4

Ingredients:

- 500 ml water
- ¼ teaspoon onion powder
- ½ teaspoon garlic powder
- 455 g radishes
- ¼ teaspoon paprika
- 2 tablespoons coconut oil, melted

Method:

1. Place water in a medium saucepan and bring to a boil on stovetop.
2. Remove the top and bottom from each radish, then use a mandoline to slice each radish thin and uniformly. You may also use the slicing blade in the food processor for this step.
3. Place the radish slices into the boiling water for 5 minutes or until translucent. Remove them from the water and place them into a clean kitchen towel to absorb excess moisture.
4. Toss the radish chips in a large bowl with remaining Ingredients until fully coated in oil and seasoning. Place radish chips into the air fryer basket.
5. Adjust the temperature to 160ºC and air fry for 5 minutes.

6. Shake the basket two or three times during the cooking time. Serve warm.

Mashed Sweet Potato Tots

Prep time: 10 minutes
Cook time: 12 to 13 minutes per batch
Makes 18 to 24 tots

Ingredients:

- 125 g cooked mashed sweet potatoes
- ⅛ teaspoon ground cinnamon
- 2 tablespoons chopped pecans
- Salt, to taste
- Oil for misting or cooking spray
- 1 egg white, beaten
- 1 dash nutmeg
- 1½ teaspoons honey
- 60 g panko bread crumbs

Method:

1. Preheat the air fryer to 200°C.
2. In a large bowl, mix together the potatoes, egg white, cinnamon, nutmeg, pecans, honey, and salt to taste.
3. Place panko crumbs on a sheet of wax paper.
4. For each tot, use about 2 teaspoons of sweet potato mixture. To shape, drop the measure of potato mixture onto panko crumbs and push crumbs up and around potatoes to coat edges. Then turn tot over to coat other side with crumbs.
5. Mist tots with oil or cooking spray and place in air fryer basket in single layer.
6. Air fry at 200°C for 12 to 13 minutes, until browned and crispy.
7. Repeat steps 5 and 6 to cook remaining tots.

Parsnip Fries with Romesco Sauce

Prep time: 20 minutes
Cook time: 24 minutes
Serves 4

Ingredients:

Romesco Sauce:

- 1 red bell pepper, halved and seeded
- 1 (1-inch) thick slice of Italian bread, torn into pieces
- 125 g almonds, toasted
- ½ Jalapeño pepper, seeded
- 1 clove garlic
- 2 plum tomatoes, peeled and seeded (or 40 g canned crushed tomatoes)
- 1 tablespoon red wine vinegar
- ½ teaspoon salt
- Olive oil
- 1 tablespoon fresh parsley leaves
- ¼ teaspoon smoked paprika
- 185 ml olive oil

- 3 parsnips, peeled and cut into long strips
- 2 teaspoons olive oil
- Salt and freshly ground black pepper, to taste

Method:

1. Preheat the air fryer to 204°C.
2. Place the red pepper halves, cut side down, in the air fryer basket and air fry for 8 to 10 minutes, or until the skin turns black all over. Remove the pepper from the air fryer and let it cool. When it is cool enough to handle, peel the pepper.
3. Toss the torn bread and almonds with a little olive oil and air fry for 4 minutes, shaking the basket a couple times throughout the cooking time. When the bread and almonds are nicely toasted, remove them from the air fryer and let them cool for just a minute or two.
4. Combine the toasted bread, almonds, roasted red pepper, Jalapeño pepper, parsley, garlic, tomatoes, vinegar, smoked paprika and salt in a food processor or blender. Process until smooth. With the processor running, add the olive oil through the feed tube until the sauce comes together in a smooth paste that is barely pourable.
5. Toss the parsnip strips with the olive oil, salt and freshly ground black pepper and air fry at 204°C for 10 minutes, shaking the basket a couple times during the cooking process so they brown and cook evenly. Serve the parsnip fries warm with the Romesco sauce to dip into.

Garlic-Parmesan Crispy Baby Potatoes

Prep time: 10 minutes
Cook time: 15 minutes
Serves 4

Ingredients:

- Oil, for spraying
- 60 g grated Parmesan cheese, divided
- 2 teaspoons garlic granules
- ½ teaspoon salt
- ¼ teaspoon paprika
- 455 g baby potatoes
- 3 tablespoons olive oil
- ½ teaspoon onion powder
- ¼ teaspoon freshly ground black pepper
- 2 tablespoons chopped fresh parsley, for garnish

Method:

1. Line the air fryer basket with baking paper and spray lightly with oil.
2. Rinse the potatoes, pat dry with paper towels, and place in a large bowl.
3. In a small bowl, mix together 30 g Parmesan cheese, the olive oil, garlic, onion powder, salt, black pepper, and paprikPour the mixture over the potatoes and toss to coat.
4. Transfer the potatoes to the prepared basket and spread them out in an even layer, taking care to keep them from touching. You may need to work in batches, depending on the size of your air fryer.
5. Air fry at 204°C for 15 minutes, stirring after 7 to 8 minutes, or until easily pierced with a fork. Continue to cook for another 1 to 2 minutes, if needed.
6. Sprinkle with the parsley and the remaining Parmesan cheese and serve.

Garlic Roasted Broccoli

Prep time: 8 minutes
Cook time: 10 to 14 minutes
Serves 6

Ingredients:

- 1 head broccoli, cut into bite-sized florets
- 2 teaspoons minced garlic
- Sea salt and freshly ground black pepper, to taste
- 1 tablespoon freshly squeezed lemon juice
- 1 tablespoon avocado oil
- ⅛ teaspoon red pepper flakes
- ½ teaspoon lemon zest

Method:

1. In a large bowl, toss together the broccoli, avocado oil, garlic, red pepper flakes, salt, and pepper.
2. Set the air fryer to 192°C. Arrange the broccoli in a single layer in the air fryer basket, working in batches if necessary. Roast for 10 to 14 minutes, until the broccoli is lightly charred.
3. Place the florets in a medium bowl and toss with the lemon juice and lemon zest. Serve.

Chermoula-Roasted Beets

Prep time: 15 minutes
Cook time: 25 minutes
Serves 4

Ingredients:

Chermoula:

- 20 g packed fresh coriander leaves
- 6 cloves garlic, peeled
- 2 teaspoons ground cumin
- ½ to 1 teaspoon cayenne pepper
- 125 ml extra-virgin olive oil
- 10 g packed fresh parsley leaves
- 2 teaspoons smoked paprika
- 1 teaspoon ground coriander
- Pinch crushed saffron (optional)
- Kosher or coarse sea salt, to taste

Beets:

- 3 medium beetroot, trimmed, peeled, and cut into 1-inch chunks
- 2 tablespoons chopped fresh coriander
- 2 tablespoons chopped fresh parsley

Method:

1. For the chermoula: In a food processor, combine the coriander leaves, parsley, garlic, paprika, cumin, coriander, and cayenne. Pulse until coarsely chopped. Add the saffron, if using, and process until combined. With the food processor running, slowly add the olive oil in a steady stream; process until the sauce is uniform. Season to taste with salt.
2. For the beets: In a large bowl, drizzle the beetroot with 125 g the chermoula, or enough to coat. Arrange the beetroot in the air fryer basket. Set the air fryer to 192°C for 25 to minutes, or until the beetroot is tender.
3. Transfer the beetroot to a serving platter. Sprinkle with chopped coriander and parsley and serve.

Mongolian-Style Beef

Prep time: 10 minutes
Cook time: 10 minutes
Serves 4

Ingredients:

- Oil, for spraying
- 450 g flank steak, thinly sliced
- 125 g soy sauce
- 1 tablespoon minced garlic
- 125 ml water
- 30 g cornflour
- 95 g Packed light brown sugar
- 2 teaspoons toasted sesame oil
- ½ teaspoon ground ginger
- Cooked white rice or ramen noodles, for serving

Method:

1. Line the air fryer basket with baking paper and spray lightly with oil.
2. Place the cornflour in a bowl and dredge the steak until evenly coated. Shake off any excess cornflour.
3. Place the steak in the prepared basket and spray lightly with oil.
4. Roast at 200°C for 5 minutes, flip, and cook for another 5 minutes.
5. In a small saucepan, combine the brown sugar, soy sauce, sesame oil, garlic, ginger, and water and bring to a boil over medium-high heat, stirring frequently. Remove from the heat.
6. Transfer the meat to the sauce and toss until evenly coated. Let sit for about 5 minutes so the steak absorbs the flavors. Serve with white rice or ramen noodles.

Beef and Tomato Sauce Meatloaf

Prep time: 15 minutes
Cook time: 25 minutes
Serves 4

Ingredients:

- 680 g minced beef
- 60 g breadcrumbs
- 60 g grated Parmesan cheese
- 2 tablespoons chopped parsley
- 2 garlic cloves, minced
- 1 teaspoon cayenne pepper
- Cooking spray
- 250 g tomato sauce
- 2 egg whites
- 1 diced onion
- 2 tablespoons minced ginger
- ½ teaspoon dried basil
- Salt and ground black pepper, to taste

Method:

1. Preheat the air fryer to 180°C. Spritz a meatloaf pan with cooking spray.
2. Combine all the Ingredients in a large bowl. Stir to mix well.

3. Pour the meat mixture in the prepared meatloaf pan and press with a spatula to make it firm.

4. Arrange the pan in the preheated air fryer and bake for 25 minutes or until the beef is well browned.

5. Serve immediately.

Sichuan Cumin Lamb

Prep time: 30 minutes
Cook time: 10 minutes
Serves 4

Ingredients:
Lamb:

- 2 tablespoons cumin seeds
- 1 teaspoon Sichuan peppercorns, or ½ teaspoon cayenne pepper
- 450 g lamb (preferably shoulder), cut into ½ by 2-inch pieces
- 2 tablespoons vegetable oil
- 1 tablespoon minced garlic
- 1 teaspoon kosher or coarse sea salt
- 1 tablespoon light soy sauce
- 2 fresh red chillies, chopped
- ¼ teaspoon sugar

For Serving:

- 2 spring onions, chopped
- Large handful of chopped fresh coriander

Method:

1. For the lamb: In a dry skillet, toast the cumin seeds and Sichuan peppercorns (if using) over medium heat, stirring frequently, until fragrant, 1 to 2 minutes. Remove from the heat and let cool. Use a mortar and pestle to coarsely grind the toasted spices.

2. Use a fork to pierce the lamb pieces to allow the marinade to penetrate better. In a large bowl or sandwich bag, combine the toasted spices, vegetable oil, soy sauce, garlic, chillies, salt, and sugar. Add the lamb to the bag. Seal and massage to coat. Marinate at room temperature for 30 minutes.

3. Place the lamb in a single layer in the air fryer basket. Set the air fryer to 176°C for 10 minutes. Use a meat thermometer to ensure the lamb has reached an internal temperature of 64°C (medium-rare).

4. Transfer the lamb to a serving bowl. Stir in the spring onions and coriander and serve.

Air Fryer Lamb Burger

Prep time: 15 minutes
Cooking time: 10 minutes
Serves 6

Ingredients:

- 2.5kg lamb mince
- 40g sundried tomato, chopped finely
- 200ml tomato ketchup
- 80g bread crumbs (divided)

- 11ml olive oil (divided)

Method:

1. Preheat the air fryer to 375°F (190°C). Place the lamb mince into a large bowl.
2. Add in half of the onion, half of the sundried tomato, half of the bread crumbs, half of the olive oil and half of the ketchup.
3. Massage well to ensure that every piece is coated with all Ingredients.
4. Place one portion onto each cornflake ring and cook for about 10 minutes until cooked through.
5. Turn each burner half way through cooking time to ensure even cooking.

Sausage and Peppers

Prep time: 7 minutes
Cook time: 35 minutes
Serves 4

Ingredients:

- Oil, for spraying
- 910 g spicy or sweet Italian sausage links, cut into thick slices
- 4 large bell peppers of any color, seeded and cut into slices
- 1 onion, thinly sliced
- 1 tablespoon chopped fresh parsley
- 1 teaspoon dried basil
- 1 tablespoon olive oil
- 1 teaspoon dried oregano
- 1 teaspoon balsamic vinegar

Method:

1. Line the air fryer basket with baking paper and spray lightly with oil.
2. In a large bowl, combine the sausage, bell peppers, and onion.
3. In a small bowl, whisk together the olive oil, parsley, oregano, basil, and balsamic vinegar. Pour the mixture over the sausage and peppers and toss until evenly coated.
4. Using a slotted spoon, transfer the mixture to the prepared basket, taking care to drain out as much excess liquid as possible.
5. Air fry at 176°C for 20 minutes, stir, and cook for another 15 minutes, or until the sausage is browned and the juices run clear.

Bacon-Wrapped Pork Tenderloin

Prep time: 30 minutes
Cook time: 22 to 25 minutes
Serves 6

Ingredients:

- 60 g minced onion
- 125 ml hard apple cider, or apple juice

- 60 g honey
- ¼ teaspoon salt
- 910 g pork tenderloin
- 8 uncooked bacon slices
- 1 tablespoon minced garlic
- ¼ teaspoon freshly ground black pepper
- 1 to 2 tablespoons oil

Method:

1. In a medium bowl, stir together the onion, hard cider, honey, garlic, salt, and pepper. Transfer to a large sandwich bag or airtight container and add the pork. Seal the bag. Refrigerate to marinate for at least 2 hours.
2. Preheat the air fryer to 204°C. Line the air fryer basket with baking paper.
3. Remove the pork from the marinade and place it on the baking paper. Spritz with oil.
4. Cook for 15 minutes.
5. Wrap the bacon slices around the pork and secure them with toothpicks. Turn the pork roast and spritz with oil. Cook for 7 to 10 minutes more until the internal temperature reaches 64°C, depending on how well-done you like pork loin. It will continue cooking after it's removed from the fryer, so let it sit for 5 minutes before serving.

Herb-Crusted Lamb Chops

Prep time: 10 minutes
Cook time: 5 minutes
Serves 2

Ingredients:

- 1 large egg
- 30 g pork scratchings, ground to dust
- 1 tablespoon chopped fresh oregano leaves
- 1 teaspoon chopped fresh thyme leaves
- 4 (1-inch-thick) lamb chops
- 2 cloves garlic, minced
- 30 g powdered Parmesan cheese
- 1 tablespoon chopped fresh rosemary leaves
- ½ teaspoon ground black pepper

For Garnish/Serving (Optional):
- Sprigs of fresh oregano
- Sprigs of fresh thyme
- Lemon slices
- Sprigs of fresh rosemary
- Lavender flowers

Method:

1. Spray the air fryer basket with avocado oil. Preheat the air fryer to 204°C.
2. Beat the egg in a shallow bowl, add the garlic, and stir well to combine. In another shallow bowl, mix together the pork dust, Parmesan, herbs, and pepper.
3. One at a time, dip the lamb chops into the egg mixture, shake off the excess egg, and then dredge them in the Parmesan mixture. Use your hands to coat the chops well in the Parmesan mixture and form a nice crust on all sides; if necessary, dip the chops again in both the egg and the Parmesan mixture.
4. Place the lamb chops in the air fryer basket, leaving space between them, and air fry for 5

minutes, or until the internal temperature reaches 64ºC for medium doneness. Allow to rest for 10 minutes before serving.

5. Garnish with sprigs of oregano, rosemary, and thyme, and lavender flowers, if desired. Serve with lemon slices, if desired.

6. Best served fresh. Store leftovers in an airtight container in the fridge for up to 4 days. Serve chilled over a salad, or reheat in a 176ºC air fryer for 3 minutes, or until heated through.

Spaghetti Zoodles and Meatballs

Prep time: 30 minutes
Cook time: 11 to 13 minutes
Serves 6

Ingredients:

- 450 g minced beef
- 1 large egg, beaten
- 95 g Parmesan cheese
- 1 teaspoon Italian seasoning
- Avocado oil spray
- 1½ teaspoons sea salt, plus more for seasoning
- 1 teaspoon gelatin
- 2 teaspoons minced garlic
- Freshly ground black pepper, to taste
- Keto-friendly marinara sauce, for serving
- 170 g courgette noodles, made using a spiraliser or store-bought

Method:

1. Place the minced beef in a large bowl, and season with the salt.
2. Place the egg in a separate bowl and sprinkle with the gelatin. Allow to sit for 5 minutes.
3. Stir the gelatin mixture, then pour it over the minced beef. Add the Parmesan, garlic, and Italian seasoning. Season with salt and pepper.
4. Form the mixture into 1½-inch meatballs and place them on a plate; cover with plastic wrap and refrigerate for at least 1 hour or overnight.
5. Spray the meatballs with oil. Set the air fryer to 204ºC and arrange the meatballs in a single layer in the air fryer basket. Air fry for 4 minutes. Flip the meatballs and spray them with more oil. Air fry for 4 minutes more, until an instant-read thermometer reads 72ºC. Transfer the meatballs to a plate and allow them to rest.
6. While the meatballs are resting, heat the marinara in a saucepan on the stove over medium heat.
7. Place the courgette noodles in the air fryer, and cook at 204ºC for 3 to 5 minutes.
8. To serve, place the courgette noodles in serving bowls. Top with meatballs and warm marinara.

Garlic Balsamic Beef

Prep time: 30 minutes
Cook time: 8 to 10 minutes
Serves 8

Ingredients:

- 910 g topside beef
- 3 tablespoons balsamic vinegar
- 2 tablespoons olive oil
- ½ teaspoon dried hot red pepper flakes
- 3 large garlic cloves, minced
- 3 tablespoons whole grain mustard
- Sea salt and ground black pepper, to taste

Method:

1. Score both sides of the cleaned beef.
2. Thoroughly combine the remaining Ingredients; massage this mixture into the meat to coat it on all sides. Let it marinate for at least 3 hours.
3. Set the air fryer to 204°C; then cook the beef for 15 minutes. Flip it over and cook another 10 to 12 minutes. Bon appétit!

Beef Burger

Prep time: 20 minutes
Cook time: 12 minutes
Serves 4

Ingredients:

- 570 g lean minced beef
- 1 teaspoon Dijon mustard
- 1 teaspoon shallot powder
- ½ teaspoon cumin powder
- ⅓ teaspoon sea salt flakes
- 1 teaspoon celery seeds
- 1 tablespoon coconut aminos or tamari
- A few dashes of liquid smoke
- 1 clove garlic, minced
- 30 g spring onions, minced
- ⅓ teaspoon freshly cracked mixed peppercorns
- 1 teaspoon parsley flakes

Method:

1. Mix all of the above Ingredients in a bowl; knead until everything is well incorporated.
2. Shape the mixture into four patties. Next, make a shallow dip in the center of each patty to prevent them puffing up during air frying.
3. Spritz the patties on all sides using nonstick cooking spray. Cook approximately 12 minutes at 184°C.
4. Check for doneness, an instant-read thermometer should read 72°C. Bon appétit!

Bacon, Cheese and Pear Stuffed Pork

Prep time: 10 minutes
Cook time: 24 minutes
Serves 3

Ingredients:

- 4 slices bacon, chopped
- 1 tablespoon butter

- 60 g finely diced onion
- 185 g seasoned stuffing cubes
- ½ teaspoon dried thyme
- ⅛ teaspoon black pepper
- 40 g crumbled blue cheese
- Olive oil
- 80 ml chicken stock
- 1 egg, beaten
- ½ teaspoon salt
- 1 pear, finely diced
- 3 boneless center-cut pork chops (2-inch thick)
- Salt and freshly ground black pepper, to taste

Method:

1. Preheat the air fryer to 204ºC.
2. Place the bacon into the air fryer basket and air fry for 6 minutes, stirring halfway through the cooking time. Remove the bacon and set it aside on a paper towel. Pour out the grease from the bottom of the air fryer.
3. Make the stuffing: Melt the butter in a medium saucepan over medium heat on the stovetop. Add the onion and sauté for a few minutes, until it starts to soften. Add the chicken stock and simmer for 1 minute. Remove the pan from the heat and add the stuffing cubes. Stir until the stock has been absorbed. Add the egg, dried thyme, salt and freshly ground black pepper, and stir until combined. Fold in the diced pear and crumbled blue cheese.
4. Place the pork chops on a cutting board. Using the palm of your hand to hold the chop flat and steady, slice into the side of the pork chop to make a pocket in the center of the chop. Leave about an inch of chop uncut and make sure you don't cut all the way through the pork chop. Brush both sides of the pork chops with olive oil and season with salt and freshly ground black pepper. Stuff each pork chop with a third of the stuffing, packing the stuffing tightly inside the pocket.
5. Preheat the air fryer to 184ºC.
6. Spray or brush the sides of the air fryer basket with oil. Place the pork chops in the air fryer basket with the open stuffed edge of the pork chop facing the outside edges of the basket.
7. Air fry the pork chops for 18 minutes, turning the pork chops over halfway through the cooking time. When the chops are done, let them rest for 5 minutes and then transfer to a serving platter.

Pork Medallions with Radicchio and Endive Salad

Prep time: 25 minutes

Cook time: 7 minutes

Serves 4

Ingredients:

- 1 (230 g) pork tenderloin
- 30 g plain flour
- 95 g matzo meal
- 1 teaspoon dry mustard
- 1 teaspoon dried thyme
- Vegetable or canola oil, in spray bottle
- Salt and freshly ground black pepper, to taste
- 2 eggs, lightly beaten
- 1 teaspoon paprika
- 1 teaspoon garlic powder
- 1 teaspoon salt

Vinaigrette:
- 65 ml white balsamic vinegar
- 2 tablespoons agave syrup (or honey or maple syrup)
- 1 tablespoon Dijon mustard
- Juice of ½ lemon
- 2 tablespoons chopped chervil or flat-leaf parsley
- Salt and freshly ground black pepper
- 125 ml extra-virgin olive oil

Radicchio and Endive Salad:
- 1 heart romaine lettuce, torn into large pieces
- ½ head radicchio, coarsely chopped
- 2 heads endive, sliced
- 60 g cherry tomatoes, halved
- 85 g fresh Mozzarella, diced
- Salt and freshly ground black pepper, to taste

Method:

1. Slice the pork tenderloin into 1-inch slices. Using a meat pounder, pound the pork slices into thin ½-inch medallions. Generously season the pork with salt and freshly ground black pepper on both sides.
2. Set up a dredging station using three shallow dishes. Put the flour in one dish and the beaten eggs in a second dish. Combine the matzo meal, paprika, dry mustard, garlic powder, thyme and salt in a third dish.
3. Preheat the air fryer to 204°C.
4. Dredge the pork medallions in flour first and then into the beaten egg. Let the excess egg drip off and coat both sides of the medallions with the matzo meal crumb mixture. Spray both sides of the coated medallions with vegetable or canola oil.
5. Air fry the medallions in two batches at 204°C for 5 minutes. Once you have air-fried all the medallions, flip them all over and return the first batch of medallions back into the air fryer on top of the second batch. Air fry at 204°C for an additional 2 minutes.
6. While the medallions are cooking, make the salad and dressing. Whisk the white balsamic vinegar, agave syrup, Dijon mustard, lemon juice, chervil, salt and pepper together in a small bowl. Whisk in the olive oil slowly until combined and thickened.
7. Combine the romaine lettuce, radicchio, endive, cherry tomatoes, and Mozzarella cheese in a large salad bowl. Drizzle the dressing over the vegetables and toss to combine. Season with salt and freshly ground black pepper.
8. Serve the pork medallions warm on or beside the salad.

Smothered Chops

Prep time: 20 minutes
Cook time: 30 minutes

Serves 4

Ingredients:

- 4 bone-in pork chops (230 g each)
- 1½ teaspoons freshly ground black pepper, divided
- 250 g tomato purée
- 1 tablespoon sugar
- 60 g chopped onion
- 1 to 2 tablespoons oil
- 2 teaspoons salt, divided
- 1 teaspoon garlic powder
- 1½ teaspoons Italian seasoning
- 1 tablespoon cornflour
- 60 g chopped green bell pepper

Method:

1. Evenly season the pork chops with 1 teaspoon salt, 1 teaspoon pepper, and the garlic powder.
2. In a medium bowl, stir together the tomato purée, Italian seasoning, sugar, remaining 1 teaspoon of salt, and remaining ½ teaspoon of pepper.
3. In a small bowl, whisk 185 ml water and the cornflour until blended. Stir this slurry into the tomato purée, with the onion and green bell pepper. Transfer to a baking pan.
4. Preheat the air fryer to 176°C.
5. Place the sauce in the fryer and cook for 10 minutes. Stir and cook for 10 minutes more. Remove the pan and keep warm.
6. Increase the air fryer temperature to 204°C. Line the air fryer basket with baking paper.
7. Place the pork chops on the baking paper and spritz with oil.
8. Cook for 5 minutes. Flip and spritz the chops with oil and cook for 5 minutes more, until the internal temperature reaches 64°C. Serve with the tomato mixture spooned on top.

Air Fryer Chicken-Fried Steak

Prep time: 5 minutes
Cook time: 20 minutes
Serves 4

Ingredients:

- 455 g beef sirloin steak
- 1 teaspoon dried thyme
- 2 medium egg whites
- 60 g coconut flour
- 750 ml skimmed milk, divided
- 1 teaspoon dried rosemary
- 125 g chickpea crumbs
- 1 tablespoon Creole seasoning

Method:

1. In a bowl, marinate the steak in 500 ml milk for 30 to 45 minutes.
2. Remove the steak from milk, shake off the excess liquid, and season with the thyme and rosemary. Discard the milk.
3. In a shallow bowl, beat the egg whites with the remaining 250 ml milk.
4. In a separate shallow bowl, combine the chickpea crumbs, coconut flour, and seasoning.
5. Dip the steak in the egg white mixture then dredge in the chickpea crumb mixture, coating well.

6. Place the steak in the basket of an air fryer.

7. Set the air fryer to 390°F, close, and cook for 10 minutes.

8. Open the air fryer, turn the steaks, close, and cook for 10 minutes. Let rest for 5 minutes.

Herb-Roasted Beef Tips with Onions

Prep time: 5 minutes

Cook time: 10 minutes

Serves 4

Ingredients:

- 455 g rib eye steak, cubed
- 2 tablespoons olive oil
- 1 teaspoon salt
- 1 yellow onion, thinly sliced
- 2 garlic cloves, minced
- 1 tablespoon fresh oregano
- ½ teaspoon black pepper

Method:

1. Preheat the air fryer to 192ºC.

2. In a medium bowl, combine the steak, garlic, olive oil, oregano, salt, pepper, and onion. Mix until all of the beef and onion are well coated.

3. Put the seasoned steak mixture into the air fryer basket. Roast for 5 minutes. Stir and roast for 5 minutes more.

4. Let rest for 5 minutes before serving with some favorite sides.

Blackened Cajun Pork Roast

Prep time: 20 minutes

Cook time: 33 minutes

Serves 4

Ingredients:

- 910 g bone-in pork loin roast
- 30 g Cajun seasoning
- 10 g diced celery
- 1 tablespoon minced garlic
- 2 tablespoons oil
- 60 g diced onion
- 60 g diced green bell pepper

Method:

1. Cut 5 slits across the pork roast. Spritz it with oil, coating it completely. Evenly sprinkle the Cajun seasoning over the pork roast.

2. In a medium bowl, stir together the onion, celery, green bell pepper, and garlic until combined. Set aside.

3. Preheat the air fryer to 184ºC. Line the air fryer basket with baking paper.

4. Place the pork roast on the baking paper and spritz with oil.

5. Cook for 5 minutes. Flip the roast and cook for 5 minutes more. Continue to flip and cook in 5-minute increments for a total Cook time of 20 minutes.
6. Increase the air fryer temperature to 200°C.
7. Cook the roast for 8 minutes more and flip. Add the vegetable mixture to the basket and cook for a final 5 minutes. Let the roast sit for 5 minutes before serving.

Bacon-Wrapped Cheese Pork

Prep time: 10 minutes
Cook time: 20 minutes
Serves 4

Ingredients:

- 4 (1-inch-thick) boneless pork chops
- 2 (150 g) packages Boursin cheese
- 8 slices thin-cut bacon
- Avocado oil for spraying

Method:

1. Spray the air fryer basket with avocado oil. Preheat the air fryer to 204°C.
2. Place one of the chops on a cutting board. With a sharp knife held parallel to the cutting board, make a 1-inch-wide incision on the top edge of the chop. Carefully cut into the chop to form a large pocket, leaving a ½-inch border along the sides and bottom. Repeat with the other 3 chops.
3. Snip the corner of a large resealable sandwich bag to form a ¾-inch hole. Place the Boursin cheese in the bag and pipe the cheese into the pockets in the chops, dividing the cheese evenly among them.
4. Wrap 2 slices of bacon around each chop and secure the ends with toothpicks. Place the bacon-wrapped chops in the air fryer basket and cook for 10 minutes, then flip the chops and cook for another 8 to 10 minutes, until the bacon is crisp, the chops are cooked through, and the internal temperature reaches 64°C.
5. Store leftovers in an airtight container in the refrigerator for up to 3 days. Reheat in a preheated 204°C air fryer for 5 minutes, or until warmed through.

Pork Tenderloin with Avocado Lime Sauce

Prep time: 30 minutes
Cook time: 15 minutes
Serves 4

Ingredients:
Marinade:
- 125 ml lime juice

- Grated zest of 1 lime
- 2 teaspoons granulated sweetener, or ¼ teaspoon liquid sweetener
- 3 cloves garlic, minced
- 1½ teaspoons fine sea salt
- 1 teaspoon chilli powder, or more for more heat
- 1 teaspoon smoked paprika
- 455 g pork tenderloin

Avocado Lime Sauce:
- 1 medium-sized ripe avocado, roughly chopped
- 125 g full-fat sour cream (or coconut cream for dairy-free)
- Grated zest of 1 lime
- Juice of 1 lime
- 2 cloves garlic, roughly chopped
- ½ teaspoon fine sea salt
- ¼ teaspoon ground black pepper
- Chopped fresh coriander leaves, for garnish
- Lime slices, for serving
- Pico de Gallo, for serving

Method:

1. In a medium-sized casserole dish, stir together all the marinade Ingredients until well combined. Add the tenderloin and coat it well in the marinade. Cover and place in the fridge to marinate for 2 hours or overnight.
2. Spray the air fryer basket with avocado oil. Preheat the air fryer to 204°C.
3. Remove the pork from the marinade and place it in the air fryer basket. Air fry for 13 to 15 minutes, until the internal temperature of the pork is 64°C, flipping after 7 minutes. Remove the pork from the air fryer and place it on a cutting board. Allow it to rest for 8 to 10 minutes, then cut it into ½-inch-thick slices.
4. While the pork cooks, make the avocado lime sauce: Place all the sauce Ingredients in a food processor and purée until smooth. Taste and adjust the seasoning to your liking.
5. Place the pork slices on a serving platter and spoon the avocado lime sauce on top. Garnish with coriander leaves and serve with lime slices and Pico de Gallo.
6. Store leftovers in an airtight container in the fridge for up to 4 days. Reheat in a preheated 204°C air fryer for 5 minutes, or until heated through.

Aubergine Fries

Prep time: 10 minutes
Cook time: 7 to 8 minutes
Serves 4

Ingredients:

- 1 medium aubergine
- 1 teaspoon cumin
- ½ teaspoon salt
- 1 large egg
- Oil for misting or cooking spray

- 1 teaspoon ground coriander
- 1 teaspoon garlic powder
- 125 g crushed panko bread crumbs
- 2 tablespoons water

Method:

1. Peel and cut the aubergine into fat fries, ⅜- to ½-inch thick.
2. Preheat the air fryer to 200°C.
3. In a small cup, mix together the coriander, cumin, garlic, and salt.
4. Combine 1 teaspoon of the seasoning mix and panko crumbs in a shallow dish.
5. Place aubergine fries in a large bowl, sprinkle with remaining seasoning, and stir well to combine.
6. Beat eggs and water together and pour over aubergine fries. Stir to coat.
7. Remove aubergine from egg wash, shaking off excess, and roll in panko crumbs.
8. Spray with oil.
9. Place half of the fries in air fryer basket. You should have only a single layer, but it's fine if they overlap a little.
10. Cook for 5 minutes. Shake basket, mist lightly with oil, and cook 2 to 3 minutes longer, until browned and crispy.
11. Repeat step 10 to cook remaining eggplant.

Air Fryer Crab Cakes

Prep time: 20 minutes Cooking time: 10 minutes
Serves 4

Ingredients:

- 380g crab meat, picked
- 15g fresh breadcrumbs
- 1 large egg, lightly beaten
- 1 medium clove garlic, crushed or minced
- 1g salt

- 60ml canola oil, divided
- 20g onion, chopped finely
- 31g mayonnaise
- 1g ground sweet paprika

Method:

1. Blend the crab meat, canola oil, egg and mayonnaise in a large bowl then stir in the onion and garlic.
2. Pour the mixture into a food processor or blender and purée to form a smooth batter. If a blender is used, chill the mixture in an ice bath before processing.
3. Transfer the batter to a large bowl then fold in the breadcrumbs, paprika and salt until evenly blended together then shape into patties with your hands.
4. Cook the crab cakes over a medium heat outside of the air fryer for 10 minutes at 200C/400F/ Gas mark 6, turning once halfway through cooking time.

Crispy Breaded Beef Cubes

Prep time: 10 minutes
Cook time: 12 to 16 minutes
Serves 4

Ingredients:

- 450 g sirloin tip, cut into 1-inch cubes
- 185 g soft bread crumbs
- ½ teaspoon dried marjoram
- 250 g cheese pasta sauce
- 2 tablespoons olive oil

Method:

1. Preheat the air fryer to 180°C.
2. In a medium bowl, toss the beef with the pasta sauce to coat.
3. In a shallow bowl, combine the bread crumbs, oil, and marjoram, and mix well. Drop the beef cubes, one at a time, into the bread crumb mixture to coat thoroughly.
4. Air fry the beef in two batches for 6 to 8 minutes, shaking the basket once during cooking time, until the beef is at least 64°C and the outside is crisp and brown.
5. Serve hot.

Shishito Peppers with Herb Dressing

Prep time: 10 minutes
Cook time: 6 minutes
Serves 2

Ingredients: to 4

- 170 g Shishito peppers
- Kosher or coarse sea salt and freshly ground black pepper, to taste
- 125 g mayonnaise
- 2 tablespoons finely chopped fresh basil leaves
- 2 tablespoons finely chopped fresh flat-leaf parsley
- 1 tablespoon finely chopped fresh tarragon
- 1 tablespoon vegetable oil

- 1 tablespoon finely chopped fresh chives
- 1 tablespoon fresh lemon juice
- Finely grated zest of ½ lemon
- Flaky sea salt, for serving

Method:

1. Preheat the air fryer to 204ºC.
2. In a bowl, toss together the Shishitos and oil to evenly coat and season with kosher salt and black pepper. Transfer to the air fryer and air fry for 6 minutes, shaking the basket halfway through, or until the Shishitos are blistered and lightly charred.
3. Meanwhile, in a small bowl, whisk together the mayonnaise, basil, parsley, tarragon, chives, lemon zest, and lemon juice.
4. Pile the peppers on a plate, sprinkle with flaky sea salt, and serve hot with the dressing.

Carrot Chips

Prep time: 15 minutes
Cook time: 8 to 10 minutes
Serves 4

Ingredients:

- 1 tablespoon olive oil, plus more for greasing the basket
- 4 to 5 medium carrots, trimmed and thinly sliced
- 1 teaspoon seasoned salt

Method:

1. Preheat the air fryer to 200ºC. Grease the air fryer basket with the olive oil.
2. Toss the carrot slices with 1 tablespoon of olive oil and salt in a medium bowl until thoroughly coated.
3. Arrange the carrot slices in the greased basket. You may need to work in batches to avoid overcrowding.
4. Air fry for 8 to 10 minutes until the carrot slices are crisp-tender. Shake the basket once during cooking.
5. Transfer the carrot slices to a bowl and repeat with the remaining carrots.
6. Allow to cool for 5 minutes and serve.

Crunchy Tex-Mex Tortilla Chips

Prep time: 5 minutes
Cook time: 5 minutes
Serves 4

Ingredients:

- Olive oil
- ½ teaspoon ground cumin
- ½ teaspoon paprika
- ½ teaspoon salt
- ½ teaspoon chilli powder
- Pinch cayenne pepper

- 8 (6-inch) corn tortillas, each cut into 6 wedges

Method:

1. Spray fryer basket lightly with olive oil.
2. In a small bowl, combine the salt, cumin, chilli powder, paprika, and cayenne pepper.
3. Place the tortilla wedges in the air fryer basket in a single layer. Spray the tortillas lightly with oil and sprinkle with some of the seasoning mixture. You will need to cook the tortillas in batches.
4. Air fry at 192°C for 2 to 3 minutes. Shake the basket and cook until the chips are light brown and crispy, an additional 2 to 3 minutes. Watch the chips closely so they do not burn.

Lemony Endive in Curried Yogurt

Prep time: 5 minutes
Cook time: 10 minutes
Serves 6

Ingredients:

- 6 heads endive
- 3 tablespoons lemon juice
- ½ teaspoon curry powder
- 125 ml plain and fat-free yogurt
- 1 teaspoon garlic powder
- Salt and ground black pepper, to taste

Method:

1. Wash the endives, and slice them in half lengthwise.
2. In a bowl, mix together the yogurt, lemon juice, garlic powder, curry powder, salt and pepper.
3. Brush the endive halves with the marinade, coating them completely. Allow to sit for at least 30 minutes or up to 24 hours.
4. Preheat the air fryer to 160°C.
5. Put the endives in the air fryer basket and air fry for 10 minutes.
6. Serve hot.

Lemon-Pepper Chicken Drumsticks

Prep time: 30 minutes
Cook time: 30 minutes
Serves 2

Ingredients:

- 2 teaspoons freshly ground coarse black pepper
- ½ teaspoon garlic powder
- Kosher or coarse sea salt, to taste
- 1 teaspoon baking powder
- 4 chicken drumsticks (115 g each)
- 1 lemon

Method:

1. In a small bowl, stir together the pepper, baking powder, and garlic powder. Place the

drumsticks on a plate and sprinkle evenly with the baking powder mixture, turning the drumsticks so they're well coated. Let the drumsticks stand in the refrigerator for at least 1 hour or up to overnight.

2. Sprinkle the drumsticks with salt, then transfer them to the air fryer, standing them bone-end up and leaning against the wall of the air fryer basket. Air fry at 192°C until cooked through and crisp on the outside, about 30 minutes.

3. Transfer the drumsticks to a serving platter and finely grate the zest of the lemon over them while they're hot. Cut the lemon into wedges and serve with the warm drumsticks.

Cheesy Steak Fries

Prep time: 5 minutes
Cook time: 20 minutes
Serves 5

Ingredients:

- 1 (800 g) bag frozen steak-cut fries
- Salt and pepper, to taste
- 125 g shredded Mozzarella cheese
- Cooking spray
- 125 g beef gravy
- 2 spring onions, green parts only, chopped

Method:

1. Preheat the air fryer to 204°C.
2. Place the frozen steak-cut fries in the air fryer. Air fry for 10 minutes. Shake the basket and spritz the fries with cooking spray. Sprinkle with salt and pepper. Air fry for an additional 8 minutes.
3. Pour the beef gravy into a medium, microwave-safe bowl. Microwave for 30 seconds, or until the gravy is warm.
4. Sprinkle the fries with the cheese. Air fry for an additional 2 minutes, until the cheese is melted.
5. Transfer the fries to a serving dish. Drizzle the fries with gravy and sprinkle the spring onions on top for a green garnish. Serve.

Black Bean Corn Dip

Prep time: 10 minutes
Cook time: 10 minutes
Serves 4

Ingredients:

- ½ (425 g) can black beans, drained and rinsed
- 60 g chunky salsa
- 30 g shredded reduced-fat Cheddar cheese
- ½ teaspoon paprika
- ½ (425 g) can sweetcorn, drained and rinsed
- 60 g reduced-fat cream cheese, softened
- ½ teaspoon ground cumin
- Salt and freshly ground black pepper, to taste

Method:

1. Preheat the air fryer to 164°C.
2. In a medium bowl, mix together the black beans, sweetcorn, salsa, cream cheese, Cheddar cheese, cumin, and paprikSeason with salt and pepper and stir until well combined.
3. Spoon the mixture into a baking dish.
4. Place baking dish in the air fryer basket and bake until heated through, about 10 minutes.
5. Serve hot.

Golden Onion Rings

Prep time: 15 minutes

Cook time: 14 minutes per batch

Serves 4

Ingredients:

* 1 large white onion, peeled and cut into ½ to ¾-inch-thick slices
* 125 ml skimmed milk
* 125 g whole-wheat pastry flour, or plain flour
* 2 tablespoons cornflour
* ¾ teaspoon sea salt, divided
* ½ teaspoon freshly ground black pepper, divided
* ¾ teaspoon granulated garlic, divided
* 185 g whole grain bread crumbs, or gluten-free bread crumbs
* Cooking oil spray (coconut, sunflower, or safflower)
* Ketchup, for serving (optional)

Method:

1. Carefully separate the onion slices into rings—a gentle touch is important here.
2. Place the milk in a shallow bowl and set aside.
3. Make the first breading: In a medium bowl, stir together the flour, cornflour, ¼ teaspoon of salt, ¼ teaspoon of pepper, and ¼ teaspoon of granulated garlic. Set aside.
4. Make the second breading: In a separate medium bowl, stir together the bread crumbs with the remaining ½ teaspoon of salt, the remaining ½ teaspoon of garlic, and the remaining ½ teaspoon of pepper. Set aside.
5. Insert the crisper plate into the basket and the basket into the unit. Preheat the unit by selecting AIR FRY, setting the temperature to 200°C, and setting the time to 3 minutes. Select START/STOP to begin.
6. Once the unit is preheated, spray the crisper plate and the basket with cooking oil.
7. To make the onion rings, dip one ring into the milk and into the first breading mixture. Dip the ring into the milk again and back into the first breading mixture, coating thoroughly. Dip the ring into the milk one last time and then into the second breading mixture, coating thoroughly. Gently lay the onion ring in the basket. Repeat with additional rings and, as you place them into the basket, do not overlap them too much. Once all the onion rings are in the

basket, generously spray the tops with cooking oil.

8. Select AIR FRY, set the temperature to 200°C, and set the time to 14 minutes. Insert the basket into the unit. Select START/STOP to begin.

9. After 4 minutes, open the unit and spray the rings generously with cooking oil. Close the unit to resume cooking. After 3 minutes, remove the basket and spray the onion rings again. Remove the rings, turn them over, and place them back into the basket. Generously spray them again with oil. Reinsert the basket to resume cooking. After 4 minutes, generously spray the rings with oil one last time. Resume cooking for the remaining 3 minutes, or until the onion rings are very crunchy and brown.

10. When the cooking is complete, serve the hot rings with ketchup, or other sauce of choice.

Bruschetta with Basil Pesto

Prep time: 10 minutes
Cook time: 5 to 11 minutes
Serves 4

Ingredients:

- 8 slices French bread, ½ inch thick
- 125 g shredded Mozzarella cheese
- 125 g chopped grape tomatoes
- 2 tablespoons softened butter
- 125 g basil pesto
- 2 spring onions, thinly sliced

Method:

1. Preheat the air fryer to 176°C.
2. Spread the bread with the butter and place butter-side up in the air fryer basket. Bake for 3 to 5 minutes, or until the bread is light golden brown.
3. Remove the bread from the basket and top each piece with some of the cheese. Return to the basket in 2 batches and bake for 1 to 3 minutes, or until the cheese melts.
4. Meanwhile, combine the pesto, tomatoes, and spring onions in a small bowl.
5. When the cheese has melted, remove the bread from the air fryer and place on a serving plate. Top each slice with some of the pesto mixture and serve.

Stuffed Figs with Goat Cheese and Honey

Prep time: 5 minutes
Cook time: 10 minutes
Serves 4

Ingredients:

- 8 fresh figs
- ¼ teaspoon ground cinnamon
- 1 tablespoon olive oil
- 60 g goat cheese
- 1 tablespoon honey, plus more for serving

Method:

1. Preheat the air fryer to 184°C.
2. Cut the stem off of each fig.
3. Cut an X into the top of each fig, cutting halfway down the fig. Leave the base intact.
4. In a small bowl, mix together the goat cheese, cinnamon, and honey.
5. Spoon the goat cheese mixture into the cavity of each fig.
6. Place the figs in a single layer in the air fryer basket. Drizzle the olive oil over top of the figs and roast for 10 minutes.
7. Serve with an additional drizzle of honey.

Courgette Fries with Roasted Garlic Aïoli

Prep time: 20 minutes
Cook time: 12 minutes
Serves 4

Ingredients:

- 1 tablespoon vegetable oil
- ½ head green or savoy cabbage, finely shredded

Roasted Garlic Aïoli:

- 1 teaspoon roasted garlic
- 125 g mayonnaise
- 2 tablespoons olive oil
- Juice of ½ lemon
- Salt and pepper, to taste

Courgette Fries:

- 60 g plain flour
- 2 eggs, beaten
- 125 g seasoned bread crumbs
- Salt and pepper, to taste
- 1 large courgette, cut into ½-inch sticks
- Olive oil

Method:

1. Make the aïoli: Combine the roasted garlic, mayonnaise, olive oil and lemon juice in a bowl and whisk well. Season the aïoli with salt and pepper to taste.
2. Prepare the courgette fries. Create a dredging station with three shallow dishes. Place the flour in the first shallow dish and season well with salt and freshly ground black pepper. Put the beaten eggs in the second shallow dish. In the third shallow dish, combine the bread crumbs, salt and pepper. Dredge the courgette sticks, coating with flour first, then dipping them into the eggs to coat, and finally tossing in bread crumbs. Shake the dish with the bread crumbs and pat the crumbs onto the courgette sticks gently with your hands so they stick evenly.
3. Place the courgette fries on a flat surface and let them sit at least 10 minutes before air frying to let them dry out a little. Preheat the air fryer to 204°C.
4. Spray the courgette sticks with olive oil, and place them into the air fryer basket. You can air fry the courgette in two layers, placing the second layer in the opposite direction to the first. Air fry for 12 minutes turning and rotating the fries halfway through the cooking time. Spray with additional oil when you turn them over.
5. Serve courgette fries warm with the roasted garlic aïoli.

Dark Chocolate and Cranberry Granola Bars

Prep time: 5 minutes
Cook time: 15 minutes
Serves 6

Ingredients:

- 250 g certified gluten-free quick oats
- 2 tablespoons unsweetened dried cranberries
- 125 g raw honey
- ⅛ teaspoon salt
- 2 tablespoons sugar-free dark chocolate chunks
- 3 tablespoons unsweetened desiccated coconut
- 1 teaspoon ground cinnamon
- 2 tablespoons olive oil

Method:

1. Preheat the air fryer to 184°C. Line an 8-by-8-inch baking dish with baking paper that comes up the side so you can lift it out after cooking.
2. In a large bowl, mix together all of the Ingredients until well combined.
3. Press the oat mixture into the pan in an even layer.
4. Place the pan into the air fryer basket and bake for 15 minutes.
5. Remove the pan from the air fryer, and lift the granola cake out of the pan using the edges of the baking paper.
6. Allow to cool for 5 minutes before slicing into 6 equal bars.
7. Serve immediately, or wrap in plastic wrap and store at room temperature for up to 1 week.

Caramelised Onion Dip

Prep time: 5 minutes
Cook time: 30 minutes
Serves 8 to 10

Ingredients:

- 1 tablespoon butter
- 1 medium yellow onion, halved and thinly sliced
- ¼ teaspoon kosher or coarse sea salt, plus additional for seasoning
- 110 g cream cheese, softened
- 125 g sour cream
- ¼ teaspoon onion powder
- 1 tablespoon chopped fresh chives
- Black pepper, to taste
- Thick-cut potato chips or vegetable chips

Method:

1. Place the butter in a baking pan. Place the pan in the air fryer basket. Set the air fryer to 92°C for 1 minute, or until the butter is melted. Add the onions and salt to the pan.
2. Set the air fryer to 92°C for 15 minutes, or until onions are softened. Set the air fryer to 192°C

for 15 minutes, until onions are a deep golden brown, stirring two or three times during the cooking time. Let cool completely.

3. In a medium bowl, stir together the cooked onions, cream cheese, sour cream, onion powder, and chives. Season with salt and pepper. Cover and refrigerate for 2 hours to allow the flavors to blend.

4. Serve the dip with potato chips or vegetable chips.

Ranch Oyster Snack Crackers

Prep time: 3 minutes
Cook time: 12 minutes
Serves 6

Ingredients:

- Oil, for spraying
- 2 teaspoons dry ranch seasoning
- ½ teaspoon dried dill
- ½ teaspoon salt
- 65 ml olive oil
- 1 teaspoon chilli powder
- ½ teaspoon garlic granules
- 1 (255 g) bag oyster crackers

Method:

1. Preheat the air fryer to 164°C. Line the air fryer basket with baking paper and spray lightly with oil.

2. In a large bowl, mix together the olive oil, ranch seasoning, chilli powder, dill, garlic, and salt. Add the crackers and toss until evenly coated.

3. Place the mixture in the prepared basket.

4. Cook for 10 to 12 minutes, shaking or stirring every 3 to 4 minutes, or until crisp and golden brown.

Air Fryer Carrot Fries

Prep time: 20 minutes
Cooking time: 8 minutes
Serves 4

Ingredients:

- 160g potatoes, cut into wedges
- 3g salt
- 1g garlic powder
- 1g paprika powder
- 25g fresh breadcrumbs
- 0.4g freshly ground pepper
- 1.5g onion powder

Method:

1. Place the potatoes into a medium-sized bowl, then sprinkle with breadcrumbs, salt and pepper. Press down on the potatoes once more to ensure that the breadcrumbs are evenly

distributed.

2. Preheat the air fryer to 200C/400F/Gas mark 6, add a wire rack to the basket then place the wedges onto it (make sure they aren't touching each other).

3. Cook for 8 minutes at 200C/400F/Gas mark 6, then transfer to a tray or plate and serve immediately.

Lemony Pear Chips

Prep time: 15 minutes
Cook time: 9 to 13 minutes
Serves 4

Ingredients:

- 2 firm Bosc pears, cut crosswise into ⅛-inch-thick slices
- 1 tablespoon freshly squeezed lemon juice
- ½ teaspoon ground cinnamon
- ⅛ teaspoon ground cardamom

Method:

1. Preheat the air fryer to 192°C.
2. Separate the smaller stem-end pear rounds from the larger rounds with seeds. Remove the core and seeds from the larger slices. Sprinkle all slices with lemon juice, cinnamon, and cardamom.
3. Put the smaller chips into the air fryer basket. Air fry for 3 to 5 minutes, or until light golden brown, shaking the basket once during cooking. Remove from the air fryer.
4. Repeat with the larger slices, air frying for 6 to 8 minutes, or until light golden brown, shaking the basket once during cooking.
5. Remove the chips from the air fryer. Cool and serve or store in an airtight container at room temperature up for to 2 days.

Crunchy Chickpeas

Prep time: 5 minutes
Cook time: 15 to 20 minutes
Serves 4

Ingredients:

- ½ teaspoon chilli powder
- ¼ teaspoon cayenne pepper
- 1 (540 g) can chickpeas, drained and rinsed
- ½ teaspoon ground cumin
- ¼ teaspoon salt
- Cooking spray

Method:

1. Preheat the air fryer to 200°C. Lightly spritz the air fryer basket with cooking spray.

2. Mix the chilli powder, cumin, cayenne pepper, and salt in a small bowl.

3. Place the chickpeas in a medium bowl and lightly mist with cooking spray.

4. Add the spice mixture to the chickpeas and toss until evenly coated.

5. Place the chickpeas in the air fryer basket and air fry for 15 to 20 minutes, or until the chickpeas are cooked to your preferred crunchiness. Shake the basket three or four times during cooking.

6. Let the chickpeas cool for 5 minutes before serving.

Classic Spring Rolls

Prep time: 10 minutes
Cook time: 9 minutes
Makes 16 spring rolls

Ingredients:

- 4 teaspoons toasted sesame oil
- 1 tablespoon grated peeled fresh ginger
- 500 g chopped green or Savoy cabbage
- ½ teaspoon sea salt
- 6 medium garlic cloves, minced or pressed
- 250 g thinly sliced shiitake mushrooms
- 125 g grated carrot
- 16 rice paper wrappers
- Cooking oil spray (sunflower, safflower, or refined coconut)
- Gluten-free sweet and sour sauce or Thai sweet chilli sauce, for serving (optional)

Method:

1. Place a wok or sauté pan over medium heat until hot.

2. Add the sesame oil, garlic, ginger, mushrooms, cabbage, carrot, and salt. Cook for 3 to 4 minutes, stirring often, until the cabbage is lightly wilted. Remove the pan from the heat.

3. Gently run a rice paper under water. Lay it on a flat nonabsorbent surface. Place about 60 g cabbage filling in the middle. Once the wrapper is soft enough to roll, fold the bottom up over the filling, fold in the sides, and roll the wrapper all the way up. (Basically, make a tiny burrito.) 4. Repeat step 3 to make the remaining spring rolls until you have the number of spring rolls you want to cook right now (and the amount that will fit in the air fryer basket in a single layer without them touching each other). Refrigerate any leftover filling in an airtight container for about 1 week.

5. Insert the crisper plate into the basket and the basket into the unit. Preheat the unit by selecting AIR FRY, setting the temperature to 200°C, and setting the time to 3 minutes. Select START/STOP to begin.

6. Once the unit is preheated, spray the crisper plate and the basket with cooking oil. Place the spring rolls into the basket, leaving a little room between them so they don't stick to each other. Spray the top of each spring roll with cooking oil.

7. Select AIR FRY, set the temperature to 200°C, and set the time to 9 minutes. Select START/STOP to begin.

8. When the cooking is complete, the egg rolls should be crisp-ish and lightly browned. Serve immediately, plain or with a sauce of choice.

Asian Five-Spice Wings

Prep time: 30 minutes
Cook time: 13 to 15 minutes
Serves 4

Ingredients:

- 910 g chicken wings
- 2 tablespoons Chinese five-spice powder
- 125 g Asian-style salad dressing

Method:

1. Cut off wing tips and discard or freeze for stock. Cut remaining wing pieces in two at the joint.
2. Place wing pieces in a large sealable plastic bag. Pour in the Asian dressing, seal bag, and massage the marinade into the wings until well coated. Refrigerate for at least an hour.
3. Remove wings from bag, drain off excess marinade, and place wings in air fryer basket.
4. Air fry at 184ºC for 13 to 15 minutes or until juices run clear. About halfway through cooking time, shake the basket or stir wings for more even cooking.
5. Transfer cooked wings to plate in a single layer. Sprinkle half of the Chinese five-spice powder on the wings, turn, and sprinkle other side with remaining seasoning.

Old Bay Chicken Wings

Prep time: 10 minutes
Cook time: 12 to 15 minutes
Serves 4

Ingredients:

- 2 tablespoons Old Bay seasoning
- 2 teaspoons salt
- Cooking spray
- 2 teaspoons baking powder
- 910 g chicken wings, patted dry

Method:

1. Preheat the air fryer to 204ºC. Lightly spray the air fryer basket with cooking spray.
2. Combine the Old Bay seasoning, baking powder, and salt in a large sandwich bag. Add the chicken wings, seal, and shake until the wings are thoroughly coated in the seasoning mixture.
3. Lay the chicken wings in the air fryer basket in a single layer and lightly mist with cooking spray. You may need to work in batches to avoid overcrowding.
4. Air fry for 12 to 15 minutes, flipping the wings halfway through, or until the wings are lightly browned and the internal temperature reaches at least 76ºC on a meat thermometer.
5. Remove from the basket to a plate and repeat with the remaining chicken wings.
6. Serve hot.

Cinnamon and Pecan Pie

Prep time: 10 minutes
Cook time: 25 minutes
Serves 4

Ingredients:

- 1 pie case
- ¾ teaspoon vanilla extract
- 185 g maple syrup
- 3 tablespoons melted butter, divided
- 60 g chopped pecans
- ½ teaspoons cinnamon
- 2 eggs
- ⅛ teaspoon nutmeg
- 2 tablespoons sugar

Method:

1. Preheat the air fryer to 188°C.
2. In a small bowl, coat the pecans in 1 tablespoon of melted butter.
3. Transfer the pecans to the air fryer and air fry for about 10 minutes.
4. Put the pie dough in a greased pie pan and add the pecans on top.
5. In a bowl, mix the rest of the Ingredients. Pour this over the pecans.
6. Put the pan in the air fryer and bake for 25 minutes.
7. Serve immediately.

Air Fryer Pumpkin Pie

Prep time: 10 minutes
Cooking time: 45 minutes
Serves 6

Ingredients:

- 450g pumpkin
- 54g egg yolks
- 175ml milk (I used skim)
- 180g cream cheese
- 80g cream cheese
- 8ml vanilla extract
- 40g caster sugar

Method:

1. Preheat your oven to 160C. Add the pumpkin, egg yolks, 4.5ml vanilla extract and milk to a food processor and puree until smooth.
2. Pour the pureed mixture into a round cake pan (approx 8 inches) lined with parchment paper in your air fryer and cook at 170C for 15 minutes.
3. Remove from the air fryer, add the rest of the vanilla extract and cream cheese to the mixture and mix well. Increase your oven temperature to 180C and cook for another 20 minutes until golden brown on top.

Olive Oil Cake

Prep time: 10 minutes
Cook time: 30 minutes
Serves 8

- 250 g blanched finely ground almond flour
- 185 ml extra-virgin olive oil
- 1 teaspoon vanilla extract
- 5 large eggs, whisked
- 40 g granulated sweetener
- 1 teaspoon baking powder

Method:

1. In a large bowl, mix all Ingredients. Pour batter into an ungreased round nonstick baking dish.
2. Place dish into air fryer basket. Adjust the temperature to 148°C and bake for 30 minutes. The cake will be golden on top and firm in the center when done.
3. Let cake cool in dish 30 minutes before slicing and serving.

Air Fryer Banana Bread

Prep time: 10 minutes
Cooking time: 25 minutes
Serves 6

Ingredients:

For topping:

- 150g all-purpose flour
- 40g light brown sugar
- 80g unsalted butter
- 3 large eggs (beaten)
- 5ml ground cinnamon
- 2.5mls vanilla extract
- 180ml whole milk
- 4 overripe bananas

Method:

1. In a medium bowl, whisk together the flour, cinnamon, brown sugar and salt. Add the butter and mix until it resembles coarse crumbs.
2. Whisk together the milk, eggs and vanilla extract in a separate bowl until pale yellow in colour then pour into the flour/butter mixture and mix until just combined with no large lumps of flour remaining.
3. Line a tray with parchment paper and spread half of the batter on top. Mix the bananas for 10 seconds in your food processor then spread on top of batter. Cover with the remaining batter and repeat steps 2-4.
4. Transfer to your air fryer and cook at 160C for 12-15 minutes or until golden brown and cooked through after removing from the oven.

Rhubarb and Strawberry Crumble

Prep time: 10 minutes

Cook time: 12 to 17 minutes

Serves 6

Ingredients:

- 185 g sliced fresh strawberries
- 40 g granulated sugar
- 60 g whole-wheat pastry flour, or plain flour
- ½ teaspoon ground cinnamon
- 15 g sliced rhubarb
- 80 g quick-cooking oatmeal
- 30 g packed light brown sugar
- 3 tablespoons unsalted butter, melted

Method:

1. Insert the crisper plate into the basket and the basket into the unit. Preheat the unit by selecting BAKE, setting the temperature to 192°C, and setting the time to 3 minutes. Select START/STOP to begin.
2. In a 6-by-2-inch round metal baking pan, combine the strawberries, rhubarb, and granulated sugar.
3. In a medium bowl, stir together the oatmeal, flour, brown sugar, and cinnamon. Stir the melted butter into this mixture until crumbly. Sprinkle the crumble mixture over the fruit.
4. Once the unit is preheated, place the pan into the basket.
5. Select BAKE, set the temperature to 192°C, and set the time to 17 minutes. Select START/STOP to begin.
6. After about 12 minutes, check the crumble. If the fruit is bubbling and the topping is golden brown, it is done. If not, resume cooking.
7. When the cooking is complete, serve warm.

Blackberry Cobbler

Prep time: 15 minutes

Cook time: 25 to 30 minutes

Serves 6

Ingredients:

- 375 g fresh or frozen blackberries
- 1 teaspoon vanilla extract
- 125 g self-raising flour
- 220 g sugar, divided
- 8 tablespoons butter, melted
- 1 to 2 tablespoons oil

Method:

1. In a medium bowl, stir together the blackberries, 125 g sugar, and vanill2. In another medium bowl, stir together the melted butter, remaining 95 g sugar, and flour until a dough forms.
3. Spritz a baking pan with oil. Add the blackberry mixture. Crumble the flour mixture over the fruit. Cover the pan with aluminum foil.
4. Preheat the air fryer to 176°C.
5. Place the covered pan in the air fryer basket. Cook for 20 to 25 minutes until the filling is thickened.
6. Uncover the pan and cook for 5 minutes more, depending on how juicy and browned you like your cobbler. Let sit for 5 minutes before serving.

Air Fryer Tasty Orange Biscuits

Prep time: 10 minutes

Cooking time: 40 minutes

Serves 6

Ingredients:

- 140g unsalted butter, melted and slightly cooled
- 2.5mls vanilla extract
- 80g self raising flour
- 75g golden syrup
- 140g dark brown sugar
- 1 medium egg (beaten)
- 2.5mls orange oil (I used sweet orange)
- 275g oranges, peeled and segmented then zested.

Method:

1. In a mixing bowl, combine the melted butter, brown sugar and vanilla extract then beat until it's smooth and creamy in texture.
2. Whisk in the egg and combine well then add the flour, orange oil and golden syrup followed by the orange zest and mix until just combined with no large lumps of flour remaining.
3. Line a baking tray with parchment paper then spoon half of the mixture onto the tray and spread out evenly to form a thin layer (no thicker than 5mm) then repeat steps 2-3 then transfer to your air fryer.
4. Bake at 170C for 15 minutes or until cooked through after removing from the oven.
5. Increase your oven temperature to 200C and cook for another 10 minutes until golden brown on top.

Apple Hand Pies

Prep time: 15 minutes

Cook time: 25 minutes

Serves 8

Ingredients:

- 2 apples, cored and diced
- 1 teaspoon ground cinnamon
- ⅛ teaspoon ground nutmeg
- 1 teaspoon water
- Cooking oil spray
- 60 g honey
- 1 teaspoon vanilla extract
- 2 teaspoons cornflour
- 4 refrigerated piecrusts

Method:

1. Insert the crisper plate into the basket and the basket into the unit. Preheat the unit by selecting AIR FRY, setting the temperature to 204ºC, and setting the time to 3 minutes. Select START/STOP to begin.
2. In a metal bowl that fits into the basket, stir together the apples, honey, cinnamon, vanilla, and nutmeg.
3. In a small bowl, whisk the cornflour and water until the cornflour dissolves.
4. Once the unit is preheated, place the metal bowl with the apples into the basket.

5. Select AIR FRY, set the temperature to 204ºC, and set the time to 5 minutes. Select START/ STOP to begin.

6. After 2 minutes, stir the apples. Resume cooking for 2 minutes.

7. Remove the bowl and stir the cornflour mixture into the apples. Reinsert the metal bowl into the basket and resume cooking for about 30 seconds until the sauce thickens slightly.

8. When the cooking is complete, refrigerate the apples while you prepare the piecrust.

9. Cut each piecrust into 2 (4-inch) circles. You should have 8 circles of crust.

10. Lay the piecrusts on a work surface. Divide the apple filling among the piecrusts, mounding the mixture in the center of each round.

11. Fold each piecrust over so the top layer of crust is about an inch short of the bottom layer. (The edges should not meet.) Use the back of a fork to seal the edges.

13. Insert the crisper plate into the basket and the basket into the unit. Preheat the unit by selecting AIR FRY, setting the temperature to 204ºC, and setting the time to 3 minutes. Select START/STOP to begin. 13. Once the unit is preheated, spray the crisper plate with cooking oil, line the basket with baking paper, and spray it with cooking oil. Working in batches, place the hand pies into the basket in a single layer. 14. Select AIR FRY, set the temperature to 204ºC, and set the time to 10 minutes. Select START/STOP to begin. 15. When the cooking is complete, let the hand pies cool for 5 minutes before removing from the basket. 16. Repeat steps 13, 14, and 15 with the remaining pies.

Gingerbread

Prep time: 5 minutes
Cook time: 20 minutes
Makes 1 loaf

Ingredients:

- Cooking spray
- 2 tablespoons sugar
- ¼ teaspoon cinnamon
- ½ teaspoon baking soda
- 1 egg
- 125 ml buttermilk
- 1 teaspoon pure vanilla extract

- 125 g plain flour
- ¾ teaspoon ground ginger
- 1 teaspoon baking powder
- ⅛ teaspoon salt
- 60 g molasses or treacle
- 2 tablespoons oil

Method:

1. Preheat the air fryer to 164ºC.
2. Spray a baking dish lightly with cooking spray.
3. In a medium bowl, mix together all the dry Ingredients.
4. In a separate bowl, beat the egg. Add molasses, buttermilk, oil, and vanilla and stir until well mixed.
5. Pour liquid mixture into dry Ingredients and stir until well blended.
6. Pour batter into baking dish and bake at 164ºC for 20 minutes or until toothpick inserted in center of loaf comes out clean.

Lime Bars

Prep time: 10 minutes
Cook time: 33 minutes
Makes 12 bars

Ingredients:

- 185 g blanched finely ground almond flour, divided
- 4 tablespoons salted butter, melted
- 2 large eggs, whisked
- 95 g powdered sweetener, divided
- 125 ml fresh lime juice

Method:

1. In a medium bowl, mix together 125 g flour, 30 g sweetener, and butter. Press mixture into bottom of an ungreased round nonstick cake pan.
2. Place pan into air fryer basket. Adjust the temperature to 148°C and bake for 13 minutes. Crust will be brown and set in the middle when done.
3. Allow to cool in pan 10 minutes.
4. In a medium bowl, combine remaining flour, remaining sweetener, lime juice, and eggs. Pour mixture over cooled crust and return to air fryer for 20 minutes at 148°C. Top will be browned and firm when done.
5. Let cool completely in pan, about 30 minutes, then chill covered in the refrigerator 1 hour. Serve chilled.

Bananas Foster

Prep time: 5 minutes
Cook time: 7 minutes
Serves 2

Ingredients:

- 1 tablespoon unsalted butter
- 1 banana, peeled and halved lengthwise and then crosswise
- 2 tablespoons chopped pecans
- 2 tablespoons light rum
- 2 teaspoons dark brown sugar
- ⅛ teaspoon ground cinnamon
- Vanilla ice cream, for serving

Method:

1. In a baking pan, combine the butter and brown sugar. Place the pan in the air fryer basket. Set the air fryer to 176°C for 2 minutes, or until the butter and sugar are melted. Swirl to combine.
2. Add the banana pieces and pecans, turning the bananas to coat. Set the air fryer to 176°C for 5 minutes, turning the banana pieces halfway through the cooking time. Sprinkle with the cinnamon.
3. Remove the pan from the air fryer and place on an unlit stovetop for safety. Add the rum to the pan, swirling to combine it with the butter mixture. Carefully light the sauce with a long-reach lighter. Spoon the flaming sauce over the banana pieces until the flames die out.
4. Serve the warm bananas and sauce over vanilla ice cream.

Printed in Great Britain
by Amazon